P9-AFE-976

Outdoor Style

The Essence of Southwest Living

by Suzanne Pickett Martinson

NORTHLAND PUBLISHING

Page i: Easy to grow, the seeds of the common sunflower (Helianthus annuus) are edible to birds, small mammals, and humans. Page ii: A delight for the senses, this outdoor living space features a dramatic poolscape, ambient lighting, welcoming furniture, and colorful foliage. Page v: Although frost sensitive, the calla lily can thrive in the Southwest if planted under shade with some daily sunlight exposure. Pages vi-vii: The southwestern version of a wreath, a ristra (made of chiles and raffia) adorns the rustic wooden door to this home's entryway and patio.

Text © 2003 by Suzanne Pickett Martinson

All rights reserved.

This book may not be reproduced in whole or in part, by any means (with the exception of short quotes for the purpose of review), without permission of the publisher. For information, address Permissions, Northland Publishing, 2900 North Fort Valley Road, Flagstaff, Arizona 86001.

www.northlandpub.com

Composed in the United States of America
Printed in China

Edited by Tammy Gales
Designed by David Jenney & Katie Jennings
Production supervised by Donna Boyd

FIRST IMPRESSION 2003
ISBN 0-87358-841-X

07   06   05   04   03   5   4   3   2   1

Library of Congress Cataloging-in-Publication Data

Martinson, Suzanne Pickett.
        Outdoor style : the essence of southwest living / by Suzanne
Pickett Martinson.
                p.   cm.
        Includes bibliographical references and index.
        1. Gardens—Southwestern States—Design.
        2. Landscape gardening—Southwestern States.
        3. Outdoor living spaces—Southwestern States. I. Title.

SB473.M296 2003
635.9'0979—dc21   2003051331

Photography © 2003 by:

Artisan Captures, photography by David B. Moore: 22, 33, 34, 39 (Top left and Bottom left), 40 (Top left, Top right, and Bottom right), 47, 48 (Top left), 51 (Top), 55, 59, 63 (Bottom), 64, 66 (Top middle), 67, 69 (Top), 70 (Top), 74 (Top left and Bottom), 76 (Bottom left), 85, 88, 91, 93 (Top), 102 (Top right), 108, 115, 116, 118-119, 120, 121

Courtesy of Cornell Laboratory of Ornithology, photography by Isidor Jeklin: 96 (Top right and Bottom left)

Courtesy of the Desert Botanical Garden, photography by Adam Rodriguez: 96 (Top left), 97

Linda Enger: i, vi-vii, 16, 24 (Top), 26-27, 43 (Bottom), 45 (Bottom), 49 (Bottom left), 51 (Bottom), 57 (Top), 58 (Bottom), 60 (Bottom), 63 (Top), 66 (Top left), 69 (Bottom right), 78-79, 80, 82, 83, 84 (Bottom left), 90, 92, 93 (Bottom), 94 (Bottom left), 95 (Bottom), 100, 102 (Bottom left), 109

Courtesy of Est Est, Inc., photography by Tony Hernandez: x-1, 6 (Top left and Bottom), 11 (Right), 14 (Bottom), 32 (Top right), 49 (Bottom right), 66 (Top right), 76 (Top right), 81

Jeff Green: front cover, 2, 46 (Bottom), 53, 77, 103, 104 (Bottom)

Courtesy of Michael P. Johnson Design Studios Ltd., photography by Bill Timmerman: 6 (Top right), 12 (left), 38, 40 (Bottom left)

Elliot Lincis: 13 (Top left), 58 (Top left and Top right), 61 (Right), 107

Courtesy of Linthicum Custom Builders, photography by Katsuhisa Kida: 49 (Top)

Charles Mann: 4, 12 (Right), 13 (Bottom right), 29, 41, 42, 48 (Bottom), 54, 56, 57 (Bottom), 60 (Top), 61 (Left), 66 (Bottom right), 69 (Bottom left), 71, 84 (Top right), 86, 95 (Top left), 104 (Top), 112-113 (Right), 130

Courtesy of Mladick Custom Homes, photography by Epic Multimedia: viii-ix, 7, 8, 9, 10-11 (Left), 14 (Top), 24 (Bottom), 30-31, 72-73

David H. Smith: 98, 99

Christine Ten Eyck: 106

John Trotto: ii, v, 18-19, 21, 25 (Bottom), 28, 32 (Bottom left and Bottom right), 35, 39 (Middle right), 43 (Top), 45 (Top), 46 (Top), 50, 52, 62, 66 (Bottom left), 68, 75, 94 (Top right), 105, 112 (Left), 114, 117, 125, author photo

Scot Zimmerman: 15, 17, 20, 23, 25 (Top), 36, 44, 48 (Top right), 70 (Bottom), 74 (Top right), 95 (Top right), 110, back cover

To my beloved parents, husband, son, and daughter,
who continue to make it all possible.

—S P M

Contents

~

PREFACE

~

Spending time outdoors has always been one of my greatest passions. As a native Phoenician, I was fortunate enough to play outside, participate in sports, and garden with my mom throughout the year. There was always a porch to relax on, a shady tree to nap under, or a secluded spot to call my own.

As I grew up, I learned to appreciate the incredible sunsets and native wildlife that was part of my outdoor living space. Curious javelina, yipping coyotes, and occasional raccoons graciously shared their space with my family. The rapid speed of the hummingbirds and the gentle flow of the butterflies offered movement and joy to our outdoor living experience. And the sunsets continued to deepen my sense of awe.

Time has passed, but my love for the outdoors has remained strong. My husband, two children, and I now carry on the legacy of spending time outside just under the shadow of Camelback Mountain. So it was with great pleasure that I undertook this project. Learning how others create and use their outdoor spaces has been a powerful inspiration for me to continue to improve my own outdoor spaces. And the professionals who shared their time and expertise with me further fueled my desire.

My wish is for you to become inspired as well. Many of the elements needed to create a comfortable and personal outdoor space lie within your heart. Paying attention to what makes you relax and feel peaceful can result in a special space you are proud to call home.

—SUZANNE PICKETT MARTINSON

Comfortable seating and an abundance of plants and natural boulders create an engaging and intimate courtyard patio.

INTRODUCTION

~

Although the allure of spending time outdoors is not limited to those living in the Southwest, we are fortunate to have weather that permits almost year-round open-air living. Because of this luxury, the outdoors as an extension of the indoors is a design concept that works especially well in this amazing region.

Architects in the Southwest routinely create outdoor living spaces with this concept in mind. Interior designers, too, are skilled at working with the exteriors of the home, paying just as much attention to the outside of a house as to the inside. And naturally, landscape architects and designers are passionate about integrating the home and the land as smoothly as possible.

If you are interested in extending your outdoor living space but don't know where to begin, this book will offer examples, tips, and suggestions from professionals on how to get started. If you have already set the foundation for your outdoor space, perhaps some of the ideas presented here will inspire you to further personalize your space for even more enjoyment.

To help you achieve your ideal outdoor living space, topics covered in this book include identifying your goals and assessing your space; using your senses to create personal and functional outdoor areas; recognizing the important role that landscape and hardscape play in outdoor living; sharing space with native animals; and offering advice and recipes for ideal outdoor cooking and entertaining.

The desire to create a special place for ourselves amidst the blue skies, fresh air, and songs of nature is an instinctive longing that we all share. It only takes a little planning and a lot of imagination to start making your dreams come true.

The ultimate in outdoor living, this home features several patios, a pool, and comfortable seating vignettes. Strategic lighting and a unique sculpture complete the setting.

OUTER SPACES

*Inside or out? By adding elements like an oversized mirror,
attractive furniture, potted plants, and an accent rug, your
outdoor living space will be transformed.*

EXTENDING YOUR LIVING SPACE

Taking Your Lifestyle to the Open Air

~

Life has become so busy and scheduled that it has now become a priority—sometimes a necessity—to take a break, slow down, and experience it at a slower pace. With all our time demands like meetings, errands, after-school activities, home maintenance, exercise, and a host of other scheduling dilemmas, finding the time and space to take a break is often a challenge. One way to escape, at least partially, is to spend time outside. And by gathering those things around you that encourage relaxation or that engage you in a favorite hobby, your experience will be much more rewarding.

Expanding and enjoying your living space, then, is something that is not completely dependent on a large budget or an expansive piece of land. Placing two chairs and a small table on your patio facing the setting sun might be all that is needed to transport you to a tranquil state of mind. Or, perhaps, dedicating a corner of your yard for a fish pond with a gurgling fountain and a bench will satisfy your need to be close to nature. It could be that your love of cooking has prompted you to consider building an outdoor kitchen or wood-burning pizza oven to explore new culinary delights. The possibilities are endless.

In practical terms, you can think of outdoor living as a way to increase your home's square footage. In emotional terms, you can think of open-air living as a way to enrich the mind-body-soul experience. Any way you view it, by using your back patio, front porch, or outdoor kitchen for dining, playing, relaxing, or entertaining, you gain invaluable space to stretch out and create meaningful moments.

Create seating vignettes throughout your outdoor space by using favorite pieces of furniture, wall art, statuary, candles, and even weather-resistant floor lamps.

TOP LEFT: *With the same color tones of furniture and flooring, inside and outside become one when separated by glass.*
TOP RIGHT: *When opened, the expansive line of glass panels and doors extend this home's living space.*
BELOW & OPPOSITE: *Hidden sliding pocket doors, consistent flooring inside and out, and complementary interior/exterior colors and materials create a seamless transition between indoor and outdoor living.*

A Seamless Transition

~

In an effort to expand your living space to the outdoors, it is important to recognize the relationship between indoor and outdoor living. The perfect relationship is actually a combination of the two, creating space outdoors that provides indoor elements—like shelter, temperature control, comfortable seating, and personal style—that are necessary to fully enjoy the space.

"Because so many of us live in the Southwest for the warm weather, sunny skies, and casual lifestyle, we want to spend as much of our time outdoors as possible," says Nancy Christensen, managing editor/garden editor of *Phoenix Home & Garden* magazine. "But with our hot summer temperatures, cool winter nights, and shorter daylight hours (due to not turning the clocks back in Arizona, for example) we have a tendency to stay inside more than we probably would like."

Tony Sutton, Allied ASID, president and head designer of Scottsdale, Arizona-based design firm Est Est, Inc., agrees that although residents of the Southwest seek the sun and appreciate the region's unique climate, they are also looking for a refuge from the heat. Because of this, spending time outside should be as effortless as possible.

LEFT: *Multiple glass doors and subtle lighting offer enough light to fully enjoy this exterior living space at night.* ABOVE: *Glass panels and doors blur the lines between the interior and exterior, lending a spacious and open feeling to any space.*

Relaxing Outdoors
~

There are natural extensions of a home that
effortlessly encourage an open-air lifestyle. Patios,
porches, courtyards, balconies, and decks are some
of the exterior elements that are typically part of
homes when they are built. Enhancing these elements offers unlimited opportunities to really
enjoy an outdoor lifestyle.

Before making drastic changes, it is important
to spend some time outside understanding your
space to see how it works with your lifestyle and
to discover what might be needed to create your
desired atmosphere. The hour of the day and seasons of the year can affect how you will use the
space, as will your work schedule, hobbies, family
life, and entertaining calendar.

For example, you might find that your neglected roof deck is the perfect spot to watch an
awe-inspiring sunrise while writing in your journal.
Or, the back porch that is seldom used except
during the summer swim season might be exactly
the setting you need to host your monthly book
club meetings. After careful observation, you
might decide that you need a secluded courtyard
on the west side of your home to view the setting
sun over the majestic mountains while watching
your children play in the enclosed area.

Time spent assessing your lifestyle and how
you want to incorporate the outdoors into your
daily life will give you a better idea of what you
need to achieve your goals.

DEFINITIONS

Patio: an outdoor space used for dining or recreation that adjoins a residence and is often paved. Also called a terrace.

Porch: a structure attached to the exterior of a building often forming a covered entrance.

Balcony: a platform that projects from the wall of a building, usually off the ground, surrounded by a railing.

Veranda: a porch or balcony, usually roofed and often partly enclosed, extending along the outside of a building. Also called a gallery.

Courtyard: a yard or patio wholly or partly surrounded by walls or shrubbery.

Deck: a roofless, floored structure, typically with a railing, that adjoins a house.

Roof deck: a roofless, floored area, typically with a railing, that is found on the top of a house or other structure.

(www.Dictionary.com)

OPPOSITE LEFT: *A glass paneled railing surrounding this balcony is all but hidden to passersby.*
OPPOSITE RIGHT: *Filtered light from trees and lush vines provide shade in the morning for reading the paper and sipping coffee, and later for afternoon wine and cheese.* ABOVE: *These rustic wooden doors open into a spacious courtyard that features a Tuscan-style fountain.*
RIGHT: *Meals are enjoyed year-round on this rustic farm table, while often-used entertaining items are stored in the wooden hutch.*

Planning Your Outdoor Space
~

"By taking time to answer the following questions before creating your ideal outdoor space, you will ensure that your project will satisfy your needs and desires," advises design aficionado Shannon Brehmer Allsworth of Phoenix, Arizona. "Your answers will help determine your priorities and will make the process much more fun and effortless," she adds.

PLANNING QUESTIONS

How do you want to use the space—to relax, entertain, inspire, play, work, escape?

When will you use the space—morning, noon, or night?

Will the space be for a limited number of people or for entertaining large groups?

Do you plan to use the space all year or just seasonally?

What are your basic needs—shelter, lighting, furniture?

What is your budget?

Is this project something you can do yourself or do you want/need a professional involved?

How much maintenance can you handle?

What style will enhance the beauty of your home—English/formal, desert/natural, cottage, Spanish, contemporary, eclectic?

TOP: *Boulders and climbing vines are used to visually connect the patio and poolscape on this home's version of a wrap-around porch.* ABOVE: *Both the main house and guest house have access to the property's outdoor living space with an expansive pool, spa, and patio.* OPPOSITE: *Furniture that can withstand the elements and oversized comfy cushions create a patio that can be used on a year-round basis.*

Sharing Your Space
~

Entertaining is a way to celebrate friendship and life. When entertaining at home, you have the opportunity to extend an even more personal invitation by sharing your treasured outdoor living space.

Although any of your favorite outdoor spaces will work for a party, consider setting the scene in often overlooked locales. Some of the most interesting spaces to use when entertaining are the detached structures located in your yard. Ramadas, gazebos, and even pergolas—all open-sided, roof-covered structures—can become the perfect location for any occasion, and especially for small, intimate gatherings.

Situated amidst the foliage of the landscape, these freestanding structures provide needed overhead protection from the sun yet foster a sense of freedom with their open sides. Accessorized with weather-resistant curtains, canvas shades, and temperature controls, these open or semi-enclosed shelters can become virtually weatherproof and usable throughout most of year. And with nature as the backdrop, excessive decorations are not needed to convey a sense of warmth and intrigue.

Wherever you stage your event, most guests are delighted to spend time outdoors. Entertaining outside provides a more relaxed environment and one that most often elicits an immediate feeling of welcome and well-being, the perfect ambiance for a social gathering.

TOP: *This ramada can be equipped with a fan, fireplace, and all the necessities for comfortable outdoor entertaining.* ABOVE: *Place a table and chairs under this vine-covered pergola as an unexpected location for your next party.* OPPOSITE LEFT: *Vines and roses are easily trained to climb arbors.* OPPOSITE RIGHT: *Nestled amongst the foliage, this gazebo offers views of the whole yard.*

DEFINITIONS

Ramada: an open or semi-enclosed shelter designed especially to provide shade.

Gazebo: a freestanding, roofed, usually open-sided structure providing a shady resting place.

Pergola: an arbor or a passageway of columns supporting a roof of trelliswork on which climbing plants are trained to grow.

Arbor: a shady resting place often made of rustic work or latticework on which plants, such as climbing shrubs or vines, are grown.

(www.Dictionary.com)

Seeking Shelter

~

Structures like ramadas, pergolas, and gazebos create a sheltered destination for outdoor living. "They serve as catalysts for the flow of energy from indoors to outdoors, and vice versa," says environmental designer Troy Bankord, of T.M. Bankord, Inc. in Phoenix, Arizona. "They can connect separate patio or outdoor entertaining areas, creating more continuity in the garden like an extension of the home."

To Bankord, these outdoor shelters also offer a dramatic backdrop. The structural elements of the building's columns create a natural anchor for vines to grow up and across the roofline, ultimately covering the entire composition. The effect can be quite spectacular.

Because of their ability to grow quickly and profusely, Bankord suggests using Lady Banks' roses, bougainvillea, cat's claw (yellow trumpet vine), Podranea (pink trumpet vine), snail vine, fig vine, or passion vine. "Sometimes it is easiest to anchor wires around the columns to allow the plants to grow upward more readily," adds Bankord. "That way they get a good foundation and can reach the sun more directly."

Pots and other containers can be used to further add dimension to the space. "Consider choosing pots in a style conducive to the interior of your home to create continuity," recommends Bankord. To provide texture and color, try potting tropical birds of paradise, African iris, shrimp plant, ferns species, cast-iron plant, Sansevieria, golden columbine, Purple Heart, cyclamen, calla lilies, and potted herbs.

"Colorful vines, potted plants, and shady planting areas can make these outdoor spaces feel more inviting," concludes Bankord, "giving you, and your guests, a reason for lingering."

PAGES 18-19: *The open design of this ramada allows easy viewing of the ever-changing sunset while effectively shielding its occupants from the rain or sun.* OPPOSITE: *The widely spaced slatted roof of this ramada offers just enough protection from the sun while allowing climbing vines to flourish.* ABOVE: *Fragrant vines frame the ramada's entrance with views to all sides. Curtains provide additional protection from the elements.*

Adding Fresh Air to the Recipe

~

Some avid cooks insist that cooking outdoors gives them more personal satisfaction and the food more flavor than the same cooking does inside the home. The natural elements, they believe, somehow conspire to make the cooking process more exciting while contributing to an unforgettable meal.

Regardless of the reason, there is no denying that outdoor cooking has a special appeal—the smells, the sights, the sounds, the taste! All of the senses are touched when we experience the joy of cooking and the pleasure of consuming *en plein air*.

This passion for outdoor cooking has evolved from the freestanding barbecue grill to fully equipped outdoor kitchens that rival interior kitchens in space, design, and functionality. Even the single barbecue grill has come into its own, with stores dedicated to a dizzying array of styles and brands. You can add mini-refrigerators, sinks, garbage compactors, chilled wine storage, microwaves, dishwashers, filtered water, and gas lines to achieve your desired level of sophistication.

But it isn't necessary to spend a fortune on an outdoor kitchen to benefit from the pleasures of cooking outside. From roasting marshmallows over your sunken fire pit to pulling a homemade pizza out of your wood-burning pizza oven, the simple act of working outdoors to prepare a meal for the body in turn provides nourishment for the soul.

ABOVE: *Installing a gas grill on the opposite side of a gas fireplace saves space and money.* OPPOSITE: *A cook's delight, this ramada holds a grill, prep station, serving space, fireplace, and enough room to linger over a delicious meal.*

The Outdoor Kitchen
~

"The outdoor kitchen changes the way you feel about dining at home," says Mad Coyote Joe, TV host of the "The Sonoran Grill" and author of cookbooks *A Gringo's Guide to Authentic Mexican Cooking, Snack Attack,* and *The Sonoran Grill,* all by Northland Publishing. "If combined with a garden atmosphere and a view, it becomes a refuge."

Outdoor kitchens also provide the backdrop for a more enjoyable family life. "The kitchen table may be cozy, but outdoor cooking and dining offer a new level of family fun in a natural setting," he says. "There's something about getting up on Sunday morning, going outside, and making eggs Benedict for the family. We enjoy the fresh air, listen to the birds, and, best of all, we talk without the TV."

Eric Linthicum, president of Scottsdale-based Linthicum Custom Builders, agrees that outdoor kitchens have become an important feature for today's homeowners. "For most people, outdoor dining is an important part of enjoying time spent outside," he says. "Our climate allows for year-round use of the outdoor amenities traditionally used inside the home."

Outdoor kitchens can also bring a new dimension to entertaining outside. "We find our dinner guests really enjoy an outdoor dinner party," says Mad Coyote Joe, who routinely entertains outdoors at his Cave Creek, Arizona home. "Our outdoor kitchen is set up with enough counter space so everybody can help with the cooking, so everyone is involved."

TOP: *Made for entertaining, this porch houses a chef's kitchen with ample patio space for an above-ground fire pit and benches.* ABOVE: *This open-air kitchen blends effortlessly with the home's poolscape and entertaining areas.*

TOP & ABOVE: *Semi-enclosed ramadas hold full working kitchens complete with all the bells and whistles. You'll never want to cook indoors again.*

For those who seek to create an outdoor kitchen, Linthicum believes that there are no rules, just common sense. "All appliances used outside that are not weatherproof need to be protected both during and after use," he says. "And all cabinetry should be durable and weather resistant.

Also consider elements such as exposure to the sun at various times of the day and proximity to the indoor kitchen. "Don't place the kitchen in a location where the summer sun will make it impractical," he adds. "Make sure it is protected but properly vented. This will increase the time you spend in that space."

Mad Coyote Joe recommends both a sunny and shady spot for kitchen activities, particularly a patio that keeps the rain at bay. "Trust me, after you become accustomed to cooking outdoors, you will even use the outdoor kitchen on days when it's raining."

Another important consideration is determining the direction of the wind. "You don't want smoke blowing in your face while cooking, and you don't want to smoke out your family and guests," says Mad Coyote Joe.

Other recommendations include big sinks and a lot of counter space. "Refrigerators aren't necessary," he says. "Something always gets left inside. But pots full of fresh herbs and fruit or citrus trees can add a lot to the ambiance."

Both Mad Coyote Joe and Linthicum agree that stainless steel is the best material to use when it comes to the grill. "If the budget allows, choose the best quality stainless steel grill with at least four burners running front to back," says Mad Coyote Joe. "This configuration allows indirect cooking, which in turn allows you to use your grill in ways you may never have imagined. I make desserts, pizza, and bread on my grill, and we always do our Thanksgiving turkey outdoors."

Enriching Your Life
Through Living Beauty
~

Everyone needs a refuge, a place to escape from the hustle and bustle of daily life. Sometimes a vacation is necessary to save sanity, but most people can't just hop on a plane after a hassled day at work and return in time for the next morning. You can, however, create and use your outdoor spaces to provide that peaceful, calm feeling that comes with getting away from it all.

Plants, water, and wildlife are known to generate an atmosphere of serenity and replenishment. Feasting the senses on the wonder of nature will often calm you down by gently putting your worries and pressures into perspective.

Creating this Garden of Eden in your own yard may initially seem impossible. But everyone has the ability to carve out a slice of paradise within his or her own space. It doesn't have to be large. In fact, because it is meant to be a cocoon of sorts, it can be as intimate as you wish. A rose-covered arbor with a comfy bench, a chaise lounge under verdant tree branches, or a gurgling lily pond could be the tonic you need to relax without having to take a trip out of town or go to a spa.

Because everyone reacts to things differently, your space will be unique. It will serve to provide you with what you need to appreciate life. Whether your centering space offers the gift of rejuvenation, inspiration, calmness, motivation, energy, or relaxation, it is a present to cherish as you struggle to maintain balance and achieve harmony in your life.

A dramatic water sculpture is the focal point for this homeowner's pond retreat.

Breathing Space
~

Do you crave to create a secret garden? A private retreat that is yours alone? "Many of us do seek a separate environment where we can go to feel tranquil," confirms Jennie Curé, landscape architect in Cave Creek, Arizona. "It is just like when we were kids and had that secret hiding place."

Finding that special place as an adult isn't as hard as it may seem. "It doesn't have to be large, just big enough to hold a chair or a chaise and perhaps a table," says Curé. "But it does need to feel comfortable—a place where it is easy to relax and absorb the calming effect."

To locate the best area for your secret hideaway, Curé suggests paying attention to a few planning details. Check drainage from the site and spend some time in the location to make sure it is what you are seeking. "If you want a morning garden spot, make sure the sun can get through during the times you want to spend there," she says.

Surface materials for the floor—whether it be swept granite or flagstone that matches your house—should be easy to maintain. And understanding the microclimate of the space is also important so you can surround yourself with plants that flourish in that zone.

Finally, personalizing your space with items and colors that attract you will further transport you to a place of serenity. "Many times murals of scenes from a favorite vacation or childhood memory are used as focal points," says Curé. "Trickling water also helps to drown out any intrusive sounds and puts your mind at ease. Whatever it is that relaxes you, feel free to bring it into the space."

OPPOSITE: *Use neglected corners and out of the way areas to create private retreats.* ABOVE: *Dappled sunlight and the smooth sway of the hammock will lull your mind and body into relaxation.*

Showering, Soaking, and Swimming

~

There is something about water and the outdoors that appeals to the kid in everyone. Visions of plunging into cool, clear water on a hot summer's day is almost as enticing as the image of relaxing with a glass of wine in a warm, bubbly spa, or taking an invigorating early morning shower in the open air. Fortunately, these scenarios can be more than just mental pictures. Pools, spas, and even outdoor showers have become an integral part of America's outdoor living experience.

Those who use outdoor showers for their daily bathing are effusive when describing the feeling of freedom they get when cleansing in nature. And because an outdoor shower only requires a minimum amount of space, options are unlimited as to where they could be situated. Installing a shower right off the master bath can be both time-saving and cost effective. Or, if placed near the pool, it can do double-duty for after-pool rinsing. Tucked into a corner or under a shady tree, showering outdoors gives a whole new meaning to the phrase "expose yourself to nature."

Many homes in the Southwest have pools. But how often are they actually used? Depending on the weather, and if your pool is heated, swimming and life around the pool can be a year-round activity. Spas, too, give pleasure throughout the seasons. Even when not in use, pools and spas offer movement and energy to the landscape. And because of their size, these large bodies of water can provide a peaceful ambiance for everyday outdoor living and serve as built-in décor for entertaining. You don't have to physically use your pool or spa on a daily basis to receive the benefits that a shimmering body of water naturally supplies.

A pool, hot tub, misters, and an outdoor shower offer homeowners and guests many ways to enjoy their southwestern lifestyle.

So if you have a pool or spa but haven't taken advantage of them lately, perhaps it is time to get reacquainted. Try serving an unexpected dinner to your family poolside one evening and notice how the water and candlelight affect the atmosphere of the meal. Or instead of painting in your studio, set your easel and paints near the spa and perhaps the luminous body of water will inspire your art in a different direction.

Move your activities out to the water and observe the difference. It might just make you fall in love with your pool again.

RIGHT: *The pool and spa are placed close to the porch to take advantage of the overhang's protection from the sun.* BOTTOM LEFT: *The shape and size of in-ground spas are flexible, allowing them to be placed in even the smallest of spaces.* BOTTOM RIGHT: *As a favorite "room," this outdoor shower features a sink, hanging vines, artwork, and the natural beauty of the sky.*

ABOVE: *A series of water fountains that empty into the pool create energy and visual interest.* TOP RIGHT: *The gorgeous view is enhanced by the illusion created by this negative edge pool.*

Water tip: *If you have a pool or spa, consider using a cover when not in use. This could help save up to 90% of the water's evaporation.*

Going to the Spa
~

"The most important thing to think about when buying a spa is your own lifestyle," offers Joe Foster, spa consultant for Durango Stoves, Spas & More in Durango, Colorado. "A lot of times people buy for their neighbors, not themselves."

Determining the size of the tub is usually the most critical decision, says Foster. "Do you want an intimate two-seater or do you plan to entertain guests?" he asks. "It's easy to choose too big or too small. Really think about the answer."

There has also been an increased interest in spas because of their therapeutic qualities. Some spas feature strategically placed jets—pulsating, straight, and spinners—targeted at specific parts of the body for rehabilitation or to ease sore muscles.

"To create the outdoor space most conducive to your style of living, consider building steps, a deck, gazebo, or even a bar surrounding the spa," recommends Foster. "The more the spa is a part of your living space, the more you will use it. After all, what could be better than relaxing in a warm, bubbly tub, enjoying your surroundings?"

Sweet Dreams
~

Decades ago, sleeping porches were a standard part of homes throughout the country. In the Southwest, sleeping porches were especially important as the intense heat (and lack of air conditioning) in the summer led homeowners to place beds on their porches out of necessity. Many porches were screened to keep out insects and other nosey wildlife, and to provide a backdrop for wet sheets that would produce evaporative cooling when the wind blew.

Although most homes these days have air conditioning, there are still some who prefer to sleep on screened porches or sunrooms (or Arizona rooms as they are sometimes called). Reminiscent of an earlier time, sleeping close to nature has many rewards. Falling asleep to the sound of nightlife, the luminescent moon, and the twinkling stars evoke a feeling of tranquility. Awaking to the sound of singing birds and the golden glow of the sun certainly feels more natural than the harsh sounds of an alarm clock. And needless to say, the fresh air is a gift to the lungs.

Now equipped with ceiling fans, portable heaters, and other creature comforts, many sunrooms also feature canvas shades or windows for further insulation. With these amenities, the sunroom has evolved into one of the most multi-functional indoor/outdoor rooms. It is now home to everything from artist studios, playrooms, and family rooms to breakfast nooks, game rooms, and entertainment centers. But, really, all you need for an afternoon snooze is a daybed or comfy couch. The rest is up to Mother Nature.

OPPOSITE: *Fully furnished, this sunporch functions as an additional living room.*
ABOVE: *With ceiling fans for ventilation and curtains for protection from the elements and insects, this sunroom can be used to sleep, eat, or entertain.*

DEFINITIONS

Sunroom/Sun Porch: a room or an enclosed porch with glass or screened walls, or numerous windows, designed for exposure to the sun. (In Arizona, a sunroom is also called an Arizona Room.)

Sleeping Porch: a well-ventilated, usually screened porch traditionally used as occasional sleeping quarters.

(www.Dictionary.com)

Snoozin'

~

Sleeping porches in the Southwest were born out of necessity. Like many homes built in the early years of the twentieth century, those in Arizona and surrounding areas were not insulated. Exterior walls constructed with masonry or brick would absorb heat from the sun during the day and transfer that heat throughout the interior of the home. The thermodynamics of this process worked well most of the year until the climate reached the extremes of the summer months.

"Sleeping porches were created to provide some comfort during the nighttime," explains Phoenix-based architect Charles Schiffner, AIA, principal and president of Charles Schiffner & Associates. "They were created using a home's ramada or porch—an open-sided structure attached to the home's exterior wall. Sheets or canvas panels were hung from the roof structure between post or column supports."

Soaked in water, these fabric panels enveloped three sides of the porch, allowing the night breeze to blow through or past the panels. This evaporated the moisture and cooled the air within the sleeping porch. Fans were used if it was a still night.

"Sleeping porches were common throughout the Southwest until the development of the roof-mounted evaporative coolers. These cooled the home's interior and the occupants adjusted accordingly to sleep inside," adds Schiffner.

"Social changes as well as technical advancements heralded the end of the sleeping porch," says Schiffner. "With population growth and resulting security concerns, the use of the sleeping porch in its historical sense came to an end."

Nothing so stirs the senses
like a morning in the garden.
WALT WHITMAN

EXCITING THE SENSES

Functional Amenities That Feather Your Nest

~

Our bodies respond to the five senses in ways not yet completely understood. Sight, sound, touch, smell, and taste all work together to create a meaningful and lasting impression.

Fortunately, the amenities you need to feel content with your outdoor spaces are at your fingertips—shelter, temperature control, visual delights, and textures. Recognizing what those needs are can sometimes be more difficult to identify. As with planning your outdoor space, the most accurate way to determine what your senses are craving is to take some time to feel what is missing. By slowing down and becoming more in tune with the space, you will be able to relax and respond accordingly.

When in this discovery process, just remember that size is not a requirement for total sensory awareness. Even the smallest of patios or backyard nooks can provide the creature comforts of shade, a cool mist, an incredible view, the gurgling sounds of a fountain, the sweet smell of honeysuckle, and the ripe fruit of a vine pomegranate. All you need is the space.

Outdoor living provides the opportunity to have all of your senses fulfilled. And those who are the most passionate about spending time outside know that it is possible to achieve that feeling.

To appease your senses, place unique handcrafted art pieces like this metal sculpture in unexpected places throughout your outdoor living space.

Sight
~

For those who embrace outdoor living, the eyes most definitely play an integral part of enjoying the experience. And for that reason, it is important to pay as much attention to the exterior home amenities as to the interior.

Eyes are naturally responsive to light. So it is no surprise that protection from the elements of the sun, particularly the southwestern sun, is vital to spending time outdoors. Drapery, awnings, and shades filter light and offer varying degrees of sunscreen. From the simple to the elaborate, these sun shields can blend in with the surroundings or become focal points for your outdoor space.

OPPOSITE: *Subtle lighting on the home's patio doesn't detract from the views of the sculpture or the cityscape below.*
ABOVE: *This outdoor living space is a feast for the eyes with twinkle lights, spot lighting, candles, a chandelier, and a wood-burning fire.* BOTTOM LEFT: *Decorative luminarias light the way to this home's courtyard entry.* RIGHT: *Wall and accent lighting highlight this seating nook and frame the view and city beyond.*

Likewise, night lighting is necessary if you intend to spend time outside during the darker hours. Recessed lighting, wall sconces, and even outdoor table lamps are becoming popular. Candles, torches, light sticks, and decorative lanterns are available in a dizzying array of styles and colors that provide necessary and ambient lighting. Twinkle lights, typically placed in trees or amongst heavy shrubs for the holidays, can become permanent additions. And luminarias, favorite special occasion lights commonly made with brown paper bags and votive candles, create a dramatic visual delight when used to define outdoor spaces.

Many people collect art because it pleases the eyes. But why keep it inside? Many types of art require exterior placement to be fully appreciated. When placing sculptures, outdoor paintings, and climate-hardy art, consider situating the pieces where they can be viewed from both outdoors as well as indoors.

Visual elements such as color, design, and style are also components of a comfortable outdoor space. The impact of color has been studied for years. Green is soothing, yellow is inspiring, red is exciting, and blue is relaxing. What mood do you want to create in your outdoor space? The possibilities are endless.

TOP LEFT, BOTTOM LEFT, & BOTTOM RIGHT: *Contemporary art pieces and animal representations provide visual stimulation and personalization to outdoor spaces.*
TOP RIGHT: *Sculptures clustered together like these Native American figures create a dramatic impact on an outdoor setting.*

*These natural rock formations grouped
together are whimsical and full of intrigue.*

OPPOSITE: *A trompe l'oeil window scene and trailing vines painted on this otherwise blank wall give visual interest and balance to the existing doorway.*
ABOVE: *An otherwise blank, uninteresting wall is turned into a vacation for the eyes with the blue of the ocean and sky reaching endlessly.* RIGHT: *This potted palm is enhanced by the painted pot in the background, while lifelike slippers add a touch of whimsy to the setting.*

Painting a Picture
~

"The use of color and texture can greatly enhance your outdoor living space," says Lisa Dell'Osso, Paradise Valley, Arizona resident and partner with Cathedral Interiors in San Francisco, California. "And oftentimes, your garden space is a good place to express personal design desires not always available within the architectural confines of your home structure."

Color naturally impacts feelings and emotions, says Dell'Osso, so carefully selecting which colors to use outdoors is as important as choosing your indoor palette. "Color can help you define different garden rooms and set the mood as well," she adds.

Jill Helms, a Mesa, Arizona-based artist, agrees that the opportunity to use color and the decorative arts outside allows the space to become enlivened. "We respond to color and to art," she says.

Scrollwork (favorite words or a saying written in decorative form) and trompe l'oeil (a painting technique that gives an illusion of photographic reality) are some of the decorative techniques effectively used in outdoor living spaces. Faux finishings (painting methods used to resemble stone, brick, wood, or aged patinas) are also in demand.

Scottsdale, Arizona-based artist Diane Rogers says that using decorative arts to complement the outdoor living space is particularly popular for new homes where homeowners desire a more aged, charming look. "The colors can add depth to the walls and create character," she notes. "It also allows a person to express themselves."

One more hint: "It is a good idea to get a sketch of what your mural or art piece will look like," advises Helms. "That way you can see how it will evolve and make changes accordingly. Then, when it is painted, it will be more spectacular."

Shielding the Sun
~

Because sun control is so important for those in the Southwest, shade management is vital when using outdoor spaces. But the additional benefit is that these necessary elements also add to the overall outdoor design, says Suzanne Smith, Allied ASID, principal of Paradise Valley, Arizona-based Suzanne Smith Interior Design Ltd. "They can really enhance the visual aspect of the outdoor space."

Permanent shade control devices such as awnings—shade structures made of weather resistant fabric—have long been popular for their effectiveness and design. Primarily attached to exterior windows and doors, awnings are hung at specific angles and heights for maximum protection.

Likewise, outdoor drapery has become increasingly popular. Used on patios, porches, pergolas, and gazebos, curtains lend an indoor feel to an outdoor space. Outdoor drapery is flexible in its use—just open and close as desired—and can easily be replaced. It can also serve as a wind barrier when tightly secured.

Options for outdoor fabrics are unlimited, having evolved from the traditional solid colors and green and white stripes. Choosing outdoor fabrics with textures, intricate designs, and multi-hued colors can easily create a more comfortable and interesting visual experience.

Although there is some maintenance involved, Smith recommends that regular whisking with a broom and washing with a hose will prolong the life and appearance of the fabric. "Sun and weather do affect the material," she adds, "but with proper maintenance, it can last up to ten years."

OPPOSITE & TOP: *The location of your porch will determine how wide your roof slats need to be if you prefer filtered light as compared to a solid roof that will completely block the sun.* ABOVE: *A tent-like screen covers the outdoor living space and pool for maximum usage during the hot summer months.*

Touch / Feel

~

Freezing cold. Sizzling hot. Muggy, humid, stifling. Ah, just right… There is nothing that provokes a response more easily than the varying degrees of temperature. That's why air conditioners and heaters are staples in homes today, especially in the dramatic southwestern climate. And because you've become accustomed to the comfort of temperature control inside the home, it is essential to recognize the importance of comfort level when creating your outdoor spaces.

Outdoor heaters and fans have made spending time outside, even on a cold or sweltering day, possible—even enjoyable. Easy to install misting systems have further extended the time we can comfortably stay outdoors. Fire features, such as above and below ground fire pits, fireplaces, and chimineas (a freestanding fire pot made of clay used in the Southwest) instantly warm the body and the mind.

The feel of textures, too, has an impact on the subconscious. An often-washed cotton covered chair with cozy, soft pillows is more conducive to lounging than scratchy, rigid seating. Fortunately, the styles and designs of today's outdoor furniture have blurred the line between indoors and out, with fabrics such as chenille and wool becoming favorites on the porch or patio.

When choosing outdoor amenities, remember that the texture of the material and feel of the design are part of the sensory experience. If it isn't comfortable now, it never will be.

TOP & OPPOSITE: *A fire bowl or a fire pit produce heat and an overall feeling of warmth and community.*
RIGHT: *Installing a cool misting system will enable you to use your outdoor living space on even the hottest of days.*

TOP LEFT & TOP RIGHT: *Weather-resistant fabrics on metal furniture or faux wicker can withstand the elements throughout the year.* BELOW: *This often-used swing is protected by a wooden arch that is designed to encourage vine growth.*

Sitting Pretty
~

Wood, aluminum, iron, wicker, mesh, synthetic—the list is endless. With all of the many choices available in the outdoor furniture market, it is sometimes hard to make a decision on what type and style is best for your outdoor living space. To get started, take a seat and take your personal preferences into consideration.

Interior designer Jo Ann Monson, ASID, of Boulevard Home Furnishings in St. George, Utah, believes that comfort is the foremost of importance when choosing outdoor furniture. "If you plan to spend any amount of time outdoors, comfortable seating is the number one priority," she says. "From that point, maintenance and personal taste are next in line."

The ability to hold up under the elements is especially important, adds Denise Mathot, ASID, interior designer and owner of Mathot Interiors in Tucson, Arizona. "Even if you keep everything under cover, the sun, rain, dust, and wind will still indirectly affect your furnishings."

Metal and synthetic materials, such as faux wicker, are able to successfully withstand the southwestern climate, even when exposed. Wood and natural wicker extend their life when placed under a roof. Cushions made from fabrics like Sunbrella and other weather-resistant materials, are great choices for exposed pieces.

Although having "matched" sets is not required when it comes to outdoor furniture, it is suggested that the pieces and colors coordinate to create a more cohesive impression. "If using colors that blend with each other, use textures to provide interest and make a statement," offers Mathot.

When creating outdoor living spaces, both Mathot and Monson advise that you take inspiration from the natural surroundings. "Pay attention to the environment around you," says Monson. "If you live by the mountains or in the desert, using similar earth tones for your outdoor space will achieve a wonderful sense of continuity."

ABOVE: *Under a roof or not, this series of weather-resistant chaise lounges resides comfortably poolside.* BOTTOM LEFT: *Outdoor furniture under a roof can stay outside throughout the year with minimal maintenance.* BOTTOM RIGHT: *Built-in seating is made more comfortable and attractive with weather-appropriate cushions and pillows.*

Sound

~

They say the sound of nature is music to the ears—birds chirping, the wind rustling, and the pitter-patter of rain. But for some, the noises that intrude upon nature can be overwhelming—loud cars, barking dogs, and noisy neighbors. No wonder it can be hard to relax outside!

Looking back to ancient wisdom, we can find the answer, or at least a remedy, to the noises of the world—water. The sound of water naturally soothes and encourages relaxation and reflection, a reprieve for busy minds. It camouflages insults to the ears with its rhythmic melody.

Because fountains and waterfalls are thought to be healing, many people incorporate these water elements into their outdoor spaces. Small tabletop fountains can create the same respite as a dramatic two-ton rock waterfall. The key is to determine where your water feature is most needed. The rest will flow just like…water.

But if your ears would prefer Bach's symphony or the latest news report on CNN, consider equipping your outdoor space with technology. Bringing the boom box or the portable TV outside is still an option. However, the entertainment center inside the home has now moved to the great outdoors. Recessed speakers, hidden big screen televisions, and elaborate sound systems can be installed seamlessly without taking away from the peaceful outdoor ambiance.

OPPOSITE: *This pool's formal design and multiple fountainheads enhance the portico arches and trompe l'oeil panorama.* TOP: *Although contemporary in design, the earth-toned fountain looks right at home amidst the desert landscape.* BOTTOM: *This concrete waterfall is situated in the corner of the yard where the flowing sounds of water can be heard from any direction.*

Making Music
~

One of the advantages of technology is that it is always improving. In the case of outdoor sound systems, technology has become more effective and less obvious.

"There are many options for today's outdoor living spaces," says Buzz Jensen, president of Scottsdale, Arizona-based Paradise Home Entertainment. "The first step is to determine your goals when it comes to sound. Do you want it for background music, for entertainment, for public speaking?"

Once you decide how you will use the sound, creating the system or retrofitting it to your existing space is the next step. If you want to conceal your speakers, consider hiding them in the ceiling, placing them in faux rocks, or installing the four- or five-inch speaker heads within your landscape.

For outside sound systems, volume control is a big concern. Jensen says that the best way to control the volume and keep it contained is to place more speakers closer together. "This is important unless you want to share the music or television with your neighbors," he adds.

Operational keypads can be designed to control not only the volume on exterior systems, but can be tied into various other components inside. "The keypad allows you to determine which speakers you want on inside, outside, or both, and to easily switch from TV to music," notes Jensen. "It is great to have the ability to have sound flowing through the interior and exterior at the same time."

Although some might worry about the maintenance of speakers and televisions outside, Jensen says that dust and dirt don't do as much damage as rain. "Keeping your TV and non-weather-resistant speakers protected from moisture will lengthen the life of your sound equipment," he says. Sound advice, indeed.

ABOVE & OPPOSITE: *Outdoor speakers have become smaller, less obvious, and require little or no maintenance. They can also be wired to work with the home's interior sound system to produce continuous, uninterrupted sound throughout your indoor and outdoor living spaces.*

Smell

~

There is something about smell that can take you to another place and time. The whiff of scented orange blossoms can evoke treasured memories of childhood or a warm summer day. Humans have involuntary reactions to smells in ways that are hard to control. So when creating outdoor space, it is important to take smell, and your reactions to certain smells, into consideration.

Surrounding your space with aromatic plants is one way to generate pleasing smells. Mint, honeysuckle, herbs, roses—there are a tremendous number of plants that naturally scent the surrounding air. Like selecting a perfume, choosing your aromatic plants can be a pleasurable experience.

OPPOSITE: *Wisteria can be grown as trees, shrubs, or vines such as this one sprawling over a trellis-covered deck.* LEFT: *Stocks, daisies, and vibrant annuals are planted near this dining area for aroma and seasonal color.* ABOVE: *Roses have long been popular for their heavenly scent, blending in with the most lush foliage or acting as colorful accents to desert landscapes.*

What's That Smell?
~

"Fragrant plants improve our connection to nature and the rhythm of the seasons," says Carole Palmer, a University of Arizona Maricopa County Cooperative Extension Master Gardener and Arizona Herb Association member. "Fragrance has the power to transport you to another place, a memory, a fantasy."

One of the most basic elements of our existence, the sense of smell can stimulate or relax, encourage, or repel. When creating an outdoor living space using aromatic plants, Palmer recommends doing a little research before planting.

"Fragrance compatibility—it's all in the nose of the beholder. Before buying aromatic plants, people should do a 'smell test' whenever possible," says Palmer. "What is fragrant to one person might smell skunky to another."

Palmer also notes that some plants are not as fragrant unless their leaves are crushed. "Wind can stimulate fragrance, so good air circulation is helpful," she says. "If they are touchable plants, you might plant them to be close to a walkway or seating area so people can brush by them on a regular basis."

Allergies are another reason to know what you are planting. And for some, strong smells can cause headaches. Palmer also advises looking at the plant itself. Some have thorns, irritating hairs or leaves, or drop litter. She suggests planting these in out of the way areas to reduce contact.

"Everyone can relate to plants, no matter what else is going on in their lives," concludes Palmer. "Plants respond to the care we give them, and we respond to their response. Fragrance enhances that relationship. It's dynamic, therapeutic, and universal." (For a more complete list of Southwest aromatic plants see page 124.)

LEFT: *This intimate gazebo is surrounded by pleasingly-scented flowering plants.*
ABOVE: *Raised flower beds and small borders can play host to numerous types of scented flowers such as these sweetly scented sweet peas making their way up a trellis.*

Enjoying the Fruits of Your Labor

~

"Growing one's own produce nourishes the soul, builds character, and gives one a deep sense of satisfaction and achievement," says Richard Gross, secretary, editor, and co-founder of the Arizona Rare Fruit Growers and board member of the California Rare Fruit Growers. It's no wonder, then, that many people desire to nourish—and taste—favorite fruit and nuts as part of their outdoor living experience.

"Citrus is a warm climate fruit and most often associated with the Southwest," notes Gross, who is a University of Arizona Cooperative Maricopa County Extension Master Gardener and board member of the Valley of the Sun Garden Club. "It is a huge family that includes oranges, tangerines, grapefruit, tangelos, lemons, pomelo, kumquat, calamondin, and many others each with multiple cultivars (varieties) that, with nominal care, can supply the homeowner with a wide range of tasty fruit each year."

Gross adds that warm climate or subtropical fruit such as mango, loquat, guava, papaya, banana, date, starfruit, passion vine, and many others can be grown in the region as well. "With these more rare, non-native types of plants, though, special consideration needs to be given to fertilizing and watering needs," he adds. "But it is amazing how they can flourish when tended to."

Taste

~

One of the pleasures of creating outdoor space is the opportunity to grow your own food. Just imagine walking outside and picking a plump, juicy tangerine off your tree, peeling it, and plopping it into your mouth, savoring every tangy bite. Although the thought of making and tending an edible garden may seem daunting, surrounding your space with a few tasty specimens may be all you need to satisfy your craving.

Do you love citrus? Tomatoes? Pecans? Artichokes? What strikes your fancy? Many vegetables, fruit, and nut plants can be grown in pots as well as the yard. And most are easy to grow. Local nurseries, county extension offices, and garden clubs are good resources for acquiring and learning about edible garden plants and flowers that grow well in your area.

TOP: *Consider growing tomatoes, onions, corn, and assorted herbs in your outdoor space.* ABOVE: *Citrus trees thrive in the Southwest climate.*

TOP LEFT: An over-sized chess set featuring sculptures made of metal is functional, ornamental, and fun!
TOP RIGHT: This brightly painted yellow wall is the perfect backdrop for a flea market window and garden chair painted a contrasting blue. Potted red geraniums give an extra boost of color making this a unique and welcoming vignette. BELOW: Animals come to life in terra cotta planters, while whimsical tin stars dangle from above. OPPOSITE: Bring the indoors out with a comfy chair and ottoman, a hand-carved wooden couch, a mosaic coffee table, and your favorite paisleys.

The Art of Personalizing Your Outdoor Space
~

When creating meaningful space, you need look no further than yourself. Personal collections, favorite art, or inspirational mementos placed in your outdoor living spaces provide a sense of comfort that will increase your desire to spend time outside.

By including items that have a special significance in your outdoor space, you honor your personality. Free from rules about what goes with what, treasured heirlooms can stand next to flea market finds and look as if they were meant to be together. It is here, in this personal space, where signs of your true self emerge.

Gardens are a form of autobiography.
SYDNEY EDDISON

Claiming Your Space
~

When looking for unusual items to complement your outdoor garden rooms, Beverly Burch, owner of the Scottsdale, Arizona-based home and garden shop The Willows, recommends keeping three things in mind: comfort, functionality, and fun.

"It is important that your outdoor spaces be a reflection of you," says Burch. "So if fun, unexpected pieces strike your fancy, go with it!"

Vintage tables, gliders, and swings are popular garden room finds, as are urns with an Old World look and rustic chairs. "Old sinks can be used to serve iced beverages and old chairs or dressers make great planters," adds Burch.

Collections such as birdhouses, antique pottery, mosaic pieces, animal-themed topiaries, even old shoes or boots turned into flowerpots can easily be incorporated into your outdoor living design. The goal is to follow your delight and don't be afraid to make mistakes.

"A unique outdoor living space is one that goes beyond simple aesthetics to incorporate the owner's interests and personal needs," notes Lynn Town, partner of Southwest Gardener, a garden accessories shop in Phoenix, Arizona. "When a garden space is both beautiful and well-used because it fits the needs of the owner, then it is truly a special place."

Town's business partner at Southwest Gardener, Amy Carlile, agrees that outdoor living spaces have personalities and characteristics all their own. "Plants, seasons, and the wildlife that occupy a space are constantly changing and evolving, so the space grows and changes, too," states Carlile. "That's what makes the space special and interesting."

ABOVE: *Birdhouses have become collectibles as well as décor for many outdoor spaces.* LEFT: *Topiaries (bushes trimmed into decorative shapes), such as this horse and rider, add an element of surprise and amusement to exterior spaces.*
OPPOSITE LEFT: *Interesting and functional pieces of furniture are keys to your personality, as this fun-loving bench demonstrates.* OPPOSITE RIGHT: *Metal décor like these dragonflies age gracefully in the southwestern climate.*

Sometimes personal art is used to camouflage something unsightly or to take advantage of existing amenities. "People in neighborhoods of the Southwest know that two things are constant: block walls and a slight breeze," says Carlile. "Outdoor art pieces that bring a decorative element to block walls break up the monotony and can create a focal point, whether it is a charming vignette or contemporary statement."

Likewise, Carlile says wind art—such as copper spinners and wind chimes that hang from trees or the roofline, and whimsical whirligigs placed on lawns or tabletops—provide color and movement to any outdoor space.

Animal art has long been a favorite theme for outdoor spaces. "Cat art and statuary have ruled for years, but the dogs are catching up," laughs Town. "People also have a soft spot for bunnies, lizards, frogs, and birds."

"Just remember," concludes Burch, "your outdoor spaces should be a reflection of you, not someone else. Make it a true living space with your own personal touch. The added benefit is that if you like it, others will too."

Get Potted

~

"Using pots helps soften hardscapes," states Craig Pearson, owner of interior plant design firm Pearson & Company in Scottsdale, Arizona. "They also add an interesting visual element to any outdoor space."

Pearson, whose company specializes in planted pots and containers, says there is an incredible variety of pots available from around the world that will enhance any architecture. "It can provide that splash or color, either with flowers or by itself," he says. "And now you can have pots on watering systems, making them even easier to maintain."

One note to remember—potted plants need much less water in cold weather and much more in the heat and sun of summer months. Also, adequate drainage is crucial to the health of your potted plants.

OPPOSITE: *Pots are often used—planted or empty—to add warmth and interest to outdoor spaces.* ABOVE: *Placing pots within the landscape can create unexpected surprises.*
RIGHT: *This brightly colored ceramic pot once only seen inside the home makes a sophisticated statement in this outdoor space.*

THE BENEFITS OF USING POTS

~ clusters of great containers in small spaces can give the feeling of more space

~ pots also allow you to move plants around for a different look, when seasons change, or when the sun moves, creating a flexible garden

~ large, empty urns or olive jars can make a very dramatic statement

~ containers can create a spot for a large cactus surrounded by a tropical landscape, and vice versa

Balance is beautiful.
Miyoko Ohno

BALANCING THE YIN & THE YANG

Using Hardscape and Landscape
to Define Your Outdoor Spaces

~

The relationship between hardscape (outdoor structures made of hard materials like retaining walls, columns, gates, and walkways) and landscape (the use of plants) is one of endless possibility. The structure of the hardscape can provide the foundation for your outdoor living areas and become part of the landscape in its design and function.

Using both structures and plants together to delineate outdoor space requires some planning. Giving thought to your goals—whether designing a complete overhaul or a small, personal space—will help you identify which hardscapes are needed to complete your project. For example, a two-tiered retaining wall next to your patio might be the perfect place to grow heirloom roses. Or perhaps you'd love to have a meandering cobblestone walkway leading down the path to your sacred space. Knowing that both hardscape and landscape complement each other makes it easier to envision and achieve your ideal space.

The two-tiered planters—one made of flagstone and the other of natural rock—efficiently define the property's landscape while allowing a profusion of greenery and color to thrive.

Functional Hardscapes as Design Elements

~

Many times when designing an outdoor space, hardscapes are overlooked while the landscape takes center stage with its showy flowers and greenery. But because hardscapes serve important functions in an outdoor environment, it is crucial to give thought to how they will be incorporated into the overall design. And by strategically using materials like stone, metal, or wood, hardscapes become an integral part of the décor whether blending in as part of the scenery, highlighting aesthetic accents, or featuring dramatic focal points.

A gate is a gate is a gate. Or is it? Gates serve the function of separating one area from another, protecting a portion of your yard, or keeping in—or out—critters or even kids. More than that, a gate can function as an art piece, especially if handcrafted with metal in a favorite design or painted a bright contrasting red or deep purple.

TOP LEFT: *River rocks cemented to the top of this railing add an unexpected touch of nature.* TOP MIDDLE AND TOP RIGHT: *Decorative iron gates, such as these, break up the monotony of a solid wall.* BOTTOM LEFT: *Antique wooden gates lend a sense of history and intrigue when used with contemporary-styled homes.* BOTTOM RIGHT AND OPPOSITE: *Consider using the style of your home to influence the design of your gate and other hardscape elements.*

Likewise, when using walls or fences to define your property line or serve as retaining walls, consider your goal. Do you want your fencing to stand back or stand out? Walls painted in playful colors are obvious accents. Those made of natural stone or painted to match the house provide a different sense of texture and are as visible, or not, as you wish. Fences made of dried ocotillo stalks may enhance the overall desert landscaping of your outdoor space, while wrought iron, natural or painted, can blend into the surroundings.

Walkways, too, can be as noticeable or subtle as desired. A formal brick path leading to your pergola provides a different experience than the same path formed with rough-cut flagstone or even preformed cobblestone. You might consider using the same flooring material as your outdoor patio to produce a flowing, uninterrupted walkway. Or, using a contrasting material could provide just the accent you desire. Again, reviewing your overall goals will help you make these decisions.

Creating unique and functional hardscapes—from paths, retaining walls, and gates to larger structures like ramadas and arbors—can be greatly enhanced by using complementary materials that work in tandem with your home's exterior and surrounding landscape.

OPPOSITE: *Flagstone defines this pool patio and coordinates with the home's interior flooring.* TOP & BOTTOM LEFT: *A meandering path of brick pavers and squares leads the eye on a gentle journey through the yard.* BOTTOM RIGHT: *Set in sand without cement, these alternating pavers can be easily installed.*

Why Hardscape?
~

"Hardscapes can enhance your enjoyment of your outdoor living spaces, and in fact, it is often hardscapes that define and create outdoor living areas," states Julia Berman, landscape designer and owner of Julia Berman Design in Santa Fe, New Mexico. "There is little point in having a garden unless you have a way to experience it."

Balancing the composition between hardscape and landscape can be a challenge. Because hardscape is usually functional and sometimes necessary, it might be easy to overuse those elements. However, the opposite is also true.

"The importance of adding hardscapes to a landscape is that it gives weight and substance to an otherwise airy design," says Marjorie Snow, landscape designer and contractor, and owner of Marjorie Snow Landscapes in Las Vegas, Nevada. "For example, raised planters in a landscape can add a different level and dimension to an otherwise flat and generic design while serving as a functional seating area as well."

When it comes to hardscape design, thoughts are mixed. Some feel that the hardscape should be used as a natural extension of the home's architecture. Others believe that depending on the type of hardscape, it is open to discretion. For example, contrasting colors and materials are sometimes used to create a focal point or dramatic statement. It is generally agreed upon, however, that when the outdoor living space is further away from the home, anything goes.

ABOVE: *By covering this bridge with large river rocks, it becomes a focal point for the landscape as well as a functional crossing over a flowing pond.*

LEFT: *A railing made of twisted twigs lends a carefree appearance to this bridge.*

OPPOSITE: *The randomly placed flagstone patio works well with the rough textured wooden entry gate and towering sunflowers.*

In the Heat of the Moment

~

Like a community gathering place, sitting fireside
with others adds pleasure to any outdoor lifestyle.
The glow of the fire and the heat it emits are
inviting. And with comfortable seating, spending
time around the fire greatly enhances your
outdoor living experience.

"There is a tendency to gather, to congregate
around a fire," says Nancy Wagner of Nancy
Wagner/Landscape Design in Scottsdale, Arizona.
"Conversation is more relaxed and there is a
shared sense of community." Wagner believes that
there is something primal in this instinct to gather
fireside. "Our fascination with fire features and
the immediate sense of relaxation we feel when
we spend time around a fire makes a big impact,"
she says. "And when you are engaged in conversation or peaceful moments in front of a fire, you
remember those times."

Scottsdale, Arizona-based architect Michael
Higgins, owner of Higgins Architects, agrees that
the warmth and glow of a fire draws people out,
physically and conversationally. "But the key is
that it doesn't have to be a big fireplace," he explains.
"In fact, depending on the space, a much smaller
fire feature could produce a more intimate effect."

With so many fire feature options available,
making a decision can be overwhelming. Choose
your ideal location first, and then explore the
types and styles available. Do you want something
permanent, such as a traditional-style fireplace
with benches or an above-ground fire pit? Or,
would something portable make more sense, like
a mushroom-shaped propane tank heater or a clay
chiminea? Examining your lifestyle, space, and
goals will help guide you to the right decision.

---

*The engaging fire in this stacked rock fireplace invites one
and all to take a seat, relax, and converse.*

TOP LEFT: *Used nearly year-round, this gas fireplace is an integral part of the ramada with its comfortable seating and easy access to the home.* TOP RIGHT: *With a crackling fire on one side and the ripple of a pool on the other, the body and mind can fully relax and experience the moment.* BELOW: *Attached to the side of the house, this fireplace can be both subtle when not in use and an attention-getter when embers are glowing.*

If you decide to build a fireplace as a focal point for your outdoor space, consider using your home as a guide to determine which style to create. "By borrowing from elements of your home such as the exterior stucco or roof tile and incorporating them into your fireplace, you further draw the element of architecture into your outdoor living space," says Higgins. "The size of your home can also dictate the size of your fireplace."

Higgins also likes to place fire features where they are visible from inside the house. "If possible, positioning the fire feature in an area where it can be seen from inside provides an additional element of atmosphere."

Both Higgins and Wagner acknowledge that gas fire features have obvious advantages over their wood burning counterparts. "For one thing, you don't have the mess to clean up afterwards," says Higgins. "This, in turn, usually motivates people to use their fire features more often. Gas features are also easy to use, and with such convincing glowing embers from the gas logs, it is hard to tell the difference."

ABOVE: *A freestanding fireplace is set against the backdrop of a verdant green golf course and stunning mountain views.*

RIGHT: *This outdoor fireplace is located away from the house but is visually attached via freestanding columns that lead to the home's exterior.*

To Wagner, the effect of burning wood on the environment is another important reason to choose gas if at all possible. "Especially in the desert climate, the inversion layer of particulate matter is made worse by the burning of wood," she says. "In fact, many cities are now starting to require that all fire feature installations use gas. And although not all areas are equipped with gas as an option, many people are choosing gas because of its many benefits."

Adding a fire feature to your outdoor living space might also encourage you to spend more time outside when it is chilly. After all, what could be more inviting than sitting by the fire while snuggling under a blanket, sipping hot chocolate, and gazing at the stars?

Ecologically-Friendly Landscapes

~

For some, mentioning the topic of Southwest land-scape automatically brings to mind desert, cactus, rocks, and lack of water. While there is truth in that image, it is actually much more abundant and colorful. And with effective water usage, it is amazing how extraordinarily lush Southwest landscapes can become.

When creating an outdoor living space, land-scaping almost always plays a central role. Many people want their favorite plants surrounding them during their time outdoors. They might select specific trees for their shade, wildflowers for their colorful accents, or native bushes for their ability to attract hummingbirds and butterflies. Plants are naturally part of any outdoor living experience, so it is to your advantage to understand how you can incorporate them into your outdoor rooms in the most personally satisfying, and ecological, ways.

LEFT & ABOVE: *Desert-adapted landscaping is more than just rocks and sand. Colorful shade trees, native bushes, and striking cactus provide an interesting visual experience.* OPPOSITE: *Using ecologically-friendly plants in your landscape can help conserve water and attract native wildlife.*

PAGES 78-79: *A sculptured Palo Verde tree provides filtered sunlight for blooming lantana near this pond's edge.* OPPOSITE: *A collection of cacti and succulents produces an amazing show of color and texture.* BOTTOM: *Native bushes like the Brittlebush bloom year round when lightly supplemented with water during the summer months.*

Because it is recognized that landscaping constitutes about 50 percent (or more) of water consumed by the average household, many garden professionals and enthusiasts promote the landscape theory of Xeriscape, using water-thrifty plants suitable to a particular region. This concept focuses on good landscape planning, including the installation of low water-use and native plants, the addition of efficient irrigation systems, the use of mulch and soil amendments, and the planting of appropriate turf (grass) areas.

The goal is to maximize the unique climate and native landscape to its fullest potential. This can mean green, vibrant, and rich, if that is what you choose. Or, it could mean natural, seasonal, and low maintenance. Overall, it means that with careful thought and planning, the resulting landscape—native or tropical, dense or minimal—uses rainfall and supplemental water efficiently and provides plants the necessary elements needed to thrive.

Planting Your Outdoor Spaces
~

When choosing plants to accompany your outdoor spaces, consider using some of your area's native and adapted plants as part of your landscape. In addition to naturally attracting wildlife such as hummingbirds and butterflies, these plants are usually low maintenance and tend to survive the extremes of heat and cold without heavy protection.

Using area-adapted plants in your outdoor living space is also a way to honor your natural environment. "The use of native plants conveys a sense of regional identity," explains Kirti Mathura, horticulturalist at the Desert Botanical Garden in Phoenix, Arizona. "It also means that once established, native plants will be more apt to survive without excessive amounts of supplemental water."

Mathura believes that our natural plants offer comfort to our outdoor spaces in various ways. "The dappled sunlight our desert trees create during the summer months is soothing and cooling, and when they shed their foliage during the winter season, they allow warming, inviting sunlight into our garden areas," she says. "Our winter deciduous vines work in a similar fashion, many of them also providing months of bright, colorful blooms as they shade patio areas."

Mathura also advises not to forget the incredible cacti, agave, succulents, and night-blooming plants that are part of our Southwest heritage. "Many are so sculptural in form that they act as wonderful accents or focal points," she notes. "They are like living sculptures!"

Native wildflowers, too, can be cultivated and grown in our outdoor settings with great success. Although they do require a little more maintenance than most plants, they tend to thrive in difficult conditions like intense heat and sunlight and poor soil.

While some people gravitate toward natural landscapes, others favor plants that are not indigenous. It is recommended that those plants be situated in the immediate area of your outdoor living spaces where there is a chance there might be some shade protection from the harsh sun.

Tesfaye Gulilat is known for his incredibly lush landscapes. The Phoenix, Arizona-based horticulturalist and landscape designer views the garden as another room of the house, only outdoors.

"I have always enjoyed designing gardens for patios because of the microclimate it allows me to create," says Gulilat. "In this region, if you can create a microclimate, you can grow any plant you desire, provided you give it the proper care."

To achieve a microclimate, Gulilat likes to start by choosing a tree and the location with care. "Depending on the size of the outdoor living space, carefully selected trees can perform great service, sometimes making it useable year round."

If the patio or outdoor space is too small for a tree, Gulilat likes to use overhead arbors and cover them with vines that have dense summer foliage and are deciduous during the winter. "This way I can also plant vines that are not dense but are colorful during the winter," he says.

The Southwest is host to a wide variety of native, area-adapted, unusual plants. By using your imagination and the plant's shape and form, you can create a unique and personal space that inspires you to spend time outside throughout the seasons.

LEFT: *The yellow and orange leaves of the California poppy make this easy-to-grow plant a favorite throughout the Southwest.* ABOVE: *Multiple plantings of cactus make more of a visual impact than if planting just one specimen.*
OPPOSITE LEFT: *The purple hue of the Santa Rita Prickly-pear, or Purple Prickly-pear, becomes more prominent with cold weather or drought conditions.*
OPPOSITE RIGHT: *Succulents are loved for their fascinating forms, sizes, and textures, like these rosette-shaped specimens.*

Water Wise
~

"It is possible to reduce the amount of water typically used for landscaping by 50 percent with proper watering practices and careful attention to other outdoor water use (like using the hose to wash the patio or walkway)," says Cathy Rymer, Water Conservation Specialist for the Town of Gilbert, Arizona. "It is important because water is a limited resource. Our population is growing, but our water supply is finite," she adds.

Drip irrigation for flowers, shrubs, and trees is usually the preferred method of watering the landscape since emitters are run to each plant separately, therefore eliminating waste. Regular maintenance is recommended to make sure the system is working correctly and to adjust the water output according to plant needs and seasons.

"Be aware that cacti in your landscape cannot be watered the same as your trees, and trees shouldn't be watered the same as shrubs," adds Rymer. "Start with a good design and put plants with like water needs on the same valve. Ideally, trees, shrubs, turf, and cacti should have their own valves."

For turf (grass) areas, sprinkler systems can be the most water efficient source if careful attention is given to the watering frequency and to how much water is used each time.

Lucy Bradley, Maricopa County Extension Agent for Urban Horticulture at The University of Arizona Cooperative Extension in Phoenix, adds that water harvesting can be extremely helpful in reducing water costs. "Capturing rainwater from the roof and hardscapes is one way," she says. "But also consider creating contours, berms, swales, and retention barriers around your plants."

Bradley also recommends using gray water. "Redirecting water from tubs, showers, bathroom sinks, and laundry can be an efficient way to irrigate the landscape," she says. These efforts can easily be combined with watering systems to keep your outdoor spaces healthy and green.

"It has been estimated that about 90 percent of plant failure is ultimately due to improper watering," concludes Rymer. "A landscape is an investment and adds value to your home. It pays to do research. Learn to program your irrigation timer—it's easier than the VCR!"

ABOVE: *Because different plants need different amounts of water, it is recommended that turf (grass) be watered via sprinkler and that other vegetation such as flowers and trees be watered separately.* LEFT: *Drip irrigation is the preferred method of watering desert-adapted plants.*

ABOVE: *Despite their pristine colors and delicate petals, roses are sturdy and adaptable to almost any climate, particularly the Southwest. Determining what zone you are in helps to identify which roses and other plants have the best chance of survival in your area.*

Planting Tip: *Roses can have a long and beautiful life in the Southwest. Combined with native plants or set against the hardscape of a weathered fence, block wall, fancy pergola, or functional retaining wall, the look and smell of roses can transform any outdoor living space. There are many types of roses available, and they can be categorized into two main groups: Modern and Old Garden. Modern roses include hybrid teas, floribunda & polyantha, grandiflora, miniature, shrub, and climber & rambler. Old Garden roses include the once blooming gallica, damask, alba, and centifolia. Old Garden repeat blooming roses include china, tea, bourbon, noisette, and hybrid perpetual.*

What is Your Zone?
~

Sometimes people fall in love with plants that aren't suited to a particular climate. When featured in magazines and books, it is assumed that these plants will thrive in any yard. Unfortunately, that isn't always the case. To get an idea whether certain plants will work in your outdoor spaces, you first need to determine your geographical plant zone.

Sunset book's plant zone classification is one of the most widely recognized, particularly for the Southwest region. Sunset's 13 zones are determined by an area's rainfall patterns, latitude, elevation, winter lows, summer highs, humidity, length of growing season, continental air influence, and local terrain. *Sunset Western Garden Book*'s plant encyclopedia has extensive plant listings according to zones. To determine your zone, log on to www.sunset.com.

The USDA Plant Hardiness Zone system is based on an area's lowest temperatures recorded for a certain number of years. The USDA map has 11 zones and can be accessed at www.usna.usda.gov.

The American Horticultural Society (AHS) developed a USA Plant Heat-Zone map that assigns 12 geographical zones of plant tolerance for heat. Find your zone by logging on to www.ahs.org.

All three zone maps and their information complement one another. However, each system may use a different zone number for your area, so it is important to research each one separately. It isn't necessary to use all three classifications to identify plants conducive to thriving in your area, but it certainly helps to use at least one guide to eliminate costly mistakes.

INNER PEACE

Nature holds the key to our aesthetic, intellectual, cognitive, and even spiritual satisfaction.

EDWARD O. WILSON

LIVING WITH NATURE

Sharing Your Space with the Environment

~

One of the benefits of extending your outdoor living space is the opportunity you will have to spend time with nature and native wildlife. Some people are lucky to live adjacent to or in wildlife habitats, while others can design an environment to attract native species. By observing and respecting native wildlife, there is incentive to slow down, making it easier to understand and enjoy the harmony of nature.

In the Southwest, there is a bountiful supply of native wildlife—birds, butterflies, and mammals—that are unique to the environment. Existing on indigenous plants and rainfall, these creatures have become adept to living with humans and their homes. And by extending your outdoor living space, you can derive pleasure from nature and interact with it in its natural surroundings.

Butterfly and hummingbird gardens have long been popular throughout the country. Here in the Southwest, there are a large number of colorful and lively species of both. Many native and area-adapted plants attract these magnificent winged-creatures. Planting several kinds of colorful plants next to your back patio might be all the enticement they need to become a part of your outdoor environment.

Likewise, other wildlife such as rabbits, squirrels, and an array of birds grace our lives. In certain areas, you may encounter javelina, coyote, fox, bats, ringtail cats, raccoons, as well as lizards, snakes, and frogs. In other locales, mountain lions, bobcats, wolves, sheep, deer, elk, skunks, predatory birds, and even bears are frequent visitors. Some people might consider these animals pests, but should they be intrusive, designing your environment effectively could turn these pesky creatures into welcomed guests.

With lilies in bloom, the serenity of this pond inspires contemplation and relaxation.

The refreshing sounds of water, active fish, and lush vegetation have also made freshwater ponds very popular. Ponds are versatile and can be designed in any shape or form, accommodating any space. By stocking your pond with fish, frogs, flowers, and plants, it can easily become one of the favorite spots in your yard.

Living with wildlife and providing shelter and food for native species can bring joy, laughter, peace, balance, hope, and inspiration into your life.

Ponds as Places of Balance
~

Having a pond is like having your own complete ecosystem. "When the vegetation, animals, water quality, and chemistry are balanced, the world works," says passionate pond owner Dan Stough. "If something gets out of balance, it doesn't work."

For Stough, president of the Greater Phoenix (Arizona) Pond Society, ponds are also great stress relievers. "I try to always spend ten minutes in the morning just watching the fish swirling or enjoying the intricate colors of a new flower that has opened, and I arrive at work with that picture in my mind," he says. "The sound of splashing water has long been known to lower one's blood pressure and heart rate. I don't even need to listen to music on the way to work. I just remember the water."

Fish: Janitors of the Pond
~

Although most people enjoy raising fish, it is important to note that these water creatures also have an important job in the pond—they control algae and mosquito larvae. There is a wide variety of fish that can successfully thrive in a pond, including goldfish, fancy goldfish, Koi, and native species.

The size and location of your pond usually determines which type and breeds of fish to stock. As a general guideline, the space needed for a Koi pond is 2 square feet per 1 inch of fish (a typical Koi is typically thirty inches long!), but the size can be smaller if you have a highly efficient filter. If space is limited, several goldfish or native species with a variety of plants need about 2 to 3 feet in depth and plant shelves about 1 foot in depth.

RIGHT: *Fish and pond vegetation live together and create their own ecosystem.* OPPOSITE: *Secluded nooks near your pond can become places of refuge and rejuvenation.*

Pond Vegetation

~

With the exception of champion water lilies or lotus, most pond plants are available at local nurseries that specialize in pond products or at pond club exchanges. Vegetation provides shade for fish and helps to control algae. Colors and shapes are varied, and popular water plants include lotus, water lilies, bog plants, floating plants, and oxygenating plants. Pond plants can be as colorful and dramatic as any in-ground foliage and can add a new dimension of texture and shape to your outdoor living space.

What is Your Pond Style?

~

There are nearly as many options in choosing a pond style as there are in choosing the architecture or design of your home. According to Stough, almost anything is possible when it comes to creating this unique outdoor space. What appeals to you? Do you desire your pond to complement your home and garden, or do you want to create something completely different? Since there are no rules as to what style to choose, this might be the time to let your imagination take the lead.

Ponds need a certain amount of shade, particularly for the fish, so vegetation is an important element to the success of a pond.

POPULAR POND STYLES

Formal: European or Middle Eastern accents, regal, flamboyant, conspicuous, symmetric curves, hard edges, corners, patterns

Contemporary Architectural: Frank Lloyd Wright-inspired, integrated into a residence, office, or other structure, stepped pools, weirs, cascades, moats, fountains, bubblers, as varied as the imagination of the designer or landscape architect

Container Gardens: oak barrels, buckets, bathtubs, troughs, pots, or anything that holds water and fits in a small space

Koi Pond: large fish, few plants, deep and vertical sides, waterfalls for aeration, a lot of hidden technology involved

Manicured Lake: used frequently in Japanese gardens, a lot of symbolism, every item meticulously placed, varied textures, contemplative areas, bonsai trees, carved stone lamps, stepping stones, grass down to the edge

Farm Pond: these tend to be large, and some are even big enough to swim in; fish and plants are allowed to run untamed, bird islands, peninsulas, wharfs, and bridges

Waterfall Pond: a lot of water movement, plunging waterfalls, churning and splashing, streambeds, dripping springs, seeps, bogs, and border plants

Lily Pond: placid water, sunny setting, a lot of water lilies and border plantings

STOUGH'S HELPFUL POND POINTS

Don't build a pond until you have a thorough under-standing of your yard. Determine which way the wind blows to get an idea of where leaves collect.

Add only a few fish at a time, enabling them and the plants to establish a good balance before you expand your numbers. Avoid radical changes or additions.

Avoid Koi if you don't plan to spend at least half an hour daily with your pond, as these expensive, specially bred carp need a larger pond (meaning more maintenance), special water filters, and more attention (they can become very fond of their human friends).

Simplify your pond wherever possible and the stress of pond maintenance will be minimized. Set up the pond to have an efficient skimmer and a filtration system suited for your pond application. Get products that are easy to service without a lot of backbreaking labor or tools. Install them where you can easily reach them.

Visit your pond every day or as often as possible. Get a nice pad to sit on and get your hands wet. Plan on dedi-cating a weekend in the fall and the spring to take care of repotting lilies, iris, and anything else that has grown beyond the confines of a pot.

ABOVE: *Stepping stones placed across this pond enable easy access to the other side as well as the ability to clean more thoroughly.* RIGHT: *Pond plants produce some of the most intensely brilliant blooms.*

Attracting Wildlife
to Your Outdoor Space
~

"The benefit of having wildlife in your outdoor living space boils down to healthy habitat," says Keith Mellon, owner of The Wild Bird Center in Scottsdale, Arizona. Mellon believes that if you have a good habitat in your yard—healthy plants that provide food, water, and shelter—you can't keep wildlife away.

"They are attracted for the same reasons we enjoy healthy yards," Mellon says. "Nature provides the perfect balance to support life, and it is not surprising that we are all trying to plant our yards with native vegetation that mimics the beauty present in our natural surroundings. Having wildlife come and enjoy our space is like a reward for our efforts and demonstrates how good of a job we have done. And the benefit to us of being able to watch wildlife is immense. There is no more calming influence we can experience than watching nature."

ABOVE: *Shade trees and desert-adapted landscaping provide protection and food for native wildlife.*
LEFT: *Desert tortoises are insect eaters and will often hibernate in burrows during the heat of the summer. There are also a plethora of lizards indigenous to the Southwest. They are considered beneficial for the landscape, because they consume large amounts of insects that might be harmful to the garden.*

Wildlife tip: *When planning to attract wildlife, remember that the most important elements are food, water, and shelter.*

Wildlife tip: *To protect certain plants from wildlife, place chicken wire around the plant or cover it with a cloth barrier until it is well established.*

Unwanted Wildlife
~

Although Mellon believes that all forms of wildlife should be welcomed, he feels that everyone should decide in an honest manner what they cannot tolerate and plan accordingly.

"There are safe, non-lethal methods of dealing with just about any nuisance wildlife situation if people simply have the patience to discover and implement a solution," he says. "Probably the most important thing to do is to cause no harm and educate oneself. If you feed wildlife, it should be healthy food in a healthy environment. Some wildlife should not be fed and predators that become too friendly with human contact always wind up being harmed." Local county extension offices or area wildlife stores will be able to help you safely and humanely deal with any unwanted wildlife or predators.

LEFT AND TOP RIGHT: *If you want to attract more native wildlife to your outdoor living spaces, be sure to supply enough water as the wildlife will come to depend on it, particularly during the dry summer months.*
TOP LEFT: *Some plants are just too tempting to native wildlife. Use chicken wire to keep your plants protected.*

The Joy of Hummingbirds
~

"Hummingbird gardens are living gardens, not a static display," says Paradise Valley, Arizona, resident Sylvia Yoder, a hummingbird aficionado and author of *Desert Hummingbird Gardens* (1999). "The company of these amusing, feisty birds often brings a smile or outright laughter. And if you are lucky and the birds nest in the garden where you can see them, a fascinating drama will unfold."

Hummingbirds are incredible pollinators. Although red flowers are initially more attractive to these tiny winged-creatures, the concentration of sucrose in a flower's nectar is ultimately the most important aspect. When you select plants, take into account when it will bloom and for how long, especially if designing a garden to provide nectar throughout the entire year.

Yoder cites other unexpected benefits of hosting hummingbirds in the garden. The fact that they are considered "clean" birds without noticeable droppings is important to many people. Hummingbirds also need about twenty-five percent of their diet to include small insects, so they act like little pest vacuums and eliminate the need for pesticide.

For year-round pleasure, consider creating a complete hummingbird habitat with trees, shrubs, and flowers that will provide nesting sites and all the elements necessary for a happy, healthy life.

BOTTOM LEFT & OPPOSITE: *Hummingbirds are attracted to colorful, nectar-rich flowers found in many southwestern landscapes, like red hibiscus and Arizona yellow bells.* TOP LEFT: *Because their coloration is not as brilliantly marked as the males', it is sometimes hard to differentiate between the female hummingbirds of different species.* TOP RIGHT: *If you offer your neighborhood hummingbirds nectar, be sure to clean it frequently—every day in the summer.*

HUMMINGBIRD FAVORITES

Trees/Large shrubs
Arizona yellow bells (*Tecoma stans*)
Baja fairy duster (*Calliandra californica*)
Blue Palo Verde (*Cercidium floridum*)
Desert willow (*Chilopsis linearis*)

Small shrubs/perennials
Baja ruellia (*Ruellia peninsularis*)
Bird of paradise (*Caesalpinia pulcherrima*)
Chuparosa (*Justicia californica*)
Desert honeysuckle (*Anisicanthus quadrifidus var. wrightii*)
Fairy duster (*Calliandra eriophylla*)
Mexican honeysuckle (*Justicia spicigera*)

Penstemon: Parry's (*Penstemon parryi*) and Firecracker (*Penstemon eatoni*)
Red justicia/Hummingbird bush (*Justicia candicans/Justicia ovata*)
Salvia: Autumn sage (*Salvia greggii*), Mexican bush sages (*Salvia leucantha*), and Texas sage (*Salvia coccinea*)
Trailing lantana (*Lantana montevidensis*)
Wolfberry (*Lycium species*)

Cactus/Succulents
Agave (*Agave spp.*)
Aloe (*Aloe spp.*)
Ocotillo (*Fouquieria splendens*)
Red yucca (*Hesperaloe parviflora*)

CREATING YOUR HUMMINGBIRD GARDEN

Follow these tips to ensure a healthy hummingbird garden:

Identify hummingbird-friendly plants already in the garden

Add hummingbird-friendly plants to your garden space

Determine frost and heat tolerance of your site

Provide shade for many of the flowering shrubs in the warm summer months

Check that plants will provide nectar at all times during the year

Provide water for bathing (not needed for drinking because of the nectar); favorites are spray and fountains

Don't do too much at once! You want to enjoy the garden, not stress out over maintenance

Provide seating areas to enjoy the birds and the garden

Add feeders to viewing areas IF you will keep feeders clean (once a week in the winter but every 2 days in the summer) and nectar fresh for an entire season

Hummingbird Tip: To prepare hummingbird nectar, boil the water to kill bacteria. Add sugar at a 1:5 ratio (1 1/4 cups water to 1/4 cup sugar). Let cool. (Because red food coloring is not necessary to attract hummingbirds to feeders and because it has not been proven whether or not the dye is harmful to the birds, it is recommended that you do not add red food coloring to your hummingbird nectar.) To maintain hummingbird feeders, clean once a month in the winter and every day in the summer to prevent bacteria.

Butterfly Gardens
~

Who doesn't smile in delight when encountering a butterfly in the garden? The beauty and grace of the butterfly has prompted many people to create special gardens in their outdoor living spaces to attract these colorful creatures.

"Butterflies are beautiful symbols of serenity and rebirth," says Barbara Hofflander, garden naturalist at the Desert Botanical Garden in Phoenix, Arizona. "They add an aura of peace and possibility to a garden."

And because many of the natural meadows that contain plants and nectar vital to butterflies have been destroyed, Hofflander feels strongly that it is important to design residential landscapes as a replacement for those natural areas. "Nothing guarantees that a butterfly will stay in one spot, but the right mixture of plants can certainly encourage it," she adds.

Interestingly, butterflies are species specific when it comes to food. Different plants attract different butterflies. Knowing what types of butterflies live in your area will help determine which plants to include in your landscape.

As with all wildlife, butterflies also need water and shelter from predators and the elements. Shrubs and trees are great for resting during a storm and a rock in a open location is an ideal place for a butterfly to get some sun.

NATIVE SOUTHWEST BUTTERFLIES

The Southwest is home to 250 species of butterflies representing six families:

Blues, Hairstreaks, and Metalmarks *(Lycaenidae)*; Brushfoots *(Nymphalidae)*; Skippers *(Hesperiidae)*; Snouts *(Libytheidae)*; Swallowtails *(Papilionidae)*; Whites and Sulphurs *(Pieridae)*.

DESERT-ADAPTED BUTTERFLY GARDEN PLANTS

Baja fairy duster *(Caliandra californica)*

Bird of paradise *(Caesalpinia pulcherrima)*

Butterfly mist *(Ageratum corymbosum)*

Desert milkweed *(Asclepias subulata)*

Mesquite tree *(Prosopi spp.)*

Salvia *(Salvia spp.)*

Sunflowers *(Helianthus spp.)*

Trailing lantana *(Lantana montevidensis)*

Verbena *(Verbena gooddingii)*

Butterfly tip: *Butterflies are more active on windless, sunny days when temperatures are between 65 and 95 degrees Fahrenheit.*

Butterfly tip: *Pesticides will kill butterflies in their adult and larval stages. Herbicides can kill host plants. Ideally, insect-lovers like hummingbirds and reptiles should be able to take care of your pests, so you won't need to use pesticides.*

Butterfly tip: *Butterflies are attracted to mass plantings of their favorite plants, especially in colors of yellow, white, red, and purple.*

OPPOSITE: *At the Desert Botanical Garden's Butterfly Pavilion, you can see many species including the black and yellow striped Zebra Longwing, which is considered Florida's official butterfly, and the Southwest native Queen.* TOP: *The colorful Gulf Fritillary prefers warmer weather and rarely survives freezing weather conditions.* ABOVE: *The large and showy Giant Swallowtail is distinguished by the yellow dots across the wingspan that lead down to the tail.* RIGHT: *One of the most common butterflies in the Southwest is the Queen.*

CREATING SACRED SPACE

Finding Serenity Using the Outdoors as Inspiration
~

Everyone needs a private space—big, small, open, or secluded, the desire for an inner "get-away" runs deep. By choosing an outdoor space for your private retreat, the benefits of nature only add to the setting. Fresh air, growing plants, and native wildlife help provide peace and inspiration. The trickle of water, a stone statue, or a memorial tree can all serve to center the heart and allow the mind to disengage.

Although any outdoor spot can be used as sacred space, many people desire separate, designated areas that are solely dedicated to their relaxation of choice, whether that be meditation (a calm, intent consideration or contemplation), yoga (a system of exercises practiced as part of the Hindu discipline to promote control of the body and mind), tai chi (a Chinese system of physical exercises designed especially for self-defense and meditation), or simply reading, writing or napping. For some, that might mean an out-of-the-way corner of the backyard, a comfortable bench under the rose-covered arbor, the roof deck on early mornings, or a pond-side patio at dusk.

Others use herbal and medicinal plants along with symbolic objects to inspire a healing space that might include comfortable seating and a table for dining amongst the foliage. For those who desire Zen-like qualities for their space, the goal is to organize a serene, minimalist, and orderly area to eliminate distractions while seeking tranquility, perhaps using a ramada as their point of reference. And those who want to honor loved ones who have passed away often choose a favorite plant or special statue to pay tribute as a memorial, placing a bench or chair nearby to relax and spend some time in thought.

When carving out your sacred space, include items that hold special significance, such as statues, symbols, or artwork.

Depending on your comfort level and need for quiet, the best place to establish your special space is one where your distractions are limited. Take into consideration neighborhood or street noise, sun or shade preferences, proximity to your home, and other possible disruptions when identifying your personal area. And the amount of space needed for your sanctuary can be as intimate as a single hammock between two memorial trees or as generous as the porch that holds your daybed for napping, rocking chair for thinking, and telescope for stargazing.

No matter what kind of space you choose, the fact that you have taken the time to seek out an area that speaks to your heart is the first step in attaining a more peaceful life.

Seeking Sacred Space
~

"We all need sacred space," says Phoenix, Arizona-based Dr. Carl Hammerschlag, M.D., internationally recognized author, psychiatrist, speaker, and healer. "It is crucial for us to experience the awe, to realize that we are connected with something other than ourselves."

Hammerschlag, author of many books including *Healing Ceremonies* and *The Theft of the Spirit*, believes that sacred space provides the structure for us to get in touch with our feelings, "to realize that we are not on this journey alone," he adds.

Although a designated space is not necessary to experience deep emotions, having a special area limits distractions and helps you focus on the present. Creating this space outdoors offers the elements of nature to help ease you into that setting of serenity.

The space does, however, need to have some personal relevance, says Hammerschlag. "It needs to have meaning for us to make a connection," he notes, "whether that be an object or symbol or piece of nature. Whatever inspires that sense of connection, whatever keeps us in balance."

LEFT: *An arched niche (a recess in a wall) serves as a focal point as it frames a family's treasured heirloom.*
ABOVE: *Favorite pillows and the surrounding landscape encourage the homeowner to use this Asian-style pergola for seeking refuge from the hassles of daily life.*
OPPOSITE: *A Frank Lloyd Wright-inspired ramada is home to a meditation space with the elements of air, fire, and water.*

For some, symbolic objects such as stones from the Grand Canyon or a piece of bark from a favorite childhood tree might provide the connection. For others, food, instruments, smells, lights, or sacred objects serve as a reminder. Still others use no objects other than the natural plants, flowers, and trees as their inspiration.

"Different people respond to different spaces," concludes Hammerschlag. "In today's world, we don't make a lot of time to hear what our inner selves are feeling, much less thinking. If a space calls to you, sings to you, talks to you, then that is a good place to start."

TOP & RIGHT: *For many people, statues evoke feelings of awe and reverence. Used as part of your special space, statues can give direction and guidance to your contemplation.* OPPOSITE: *To establish a space that holds special significance to you, choose items that stimulate your senses, such as this European wall fountain surrounded by a tiled arch and columns. A place to sit and read or to enjoy a cup of tea completes the setting.*

OPPOSITE: *You don't need a formally designated space to spend some quiet time alone. Sometimes a simple bench placed in the midst of nature will do.* RIGHT: *Relaxed seating near a peaceful pond may be all you need to soothe your soul.*

Making Space
~

Landscape architect Greg Trutza, owner of New Directions in Landscape Architecture in Phoenix, Arizona, believes that one of the easiest ways to restore one's spirit is to spend time outdoors. "The vitality of a dynamic living environment restores the mind, body, and spirit far beyond any form of man-made entertainment," he says. "The miracle of creation changes from day to day, hour by hour. This fascination is with not only observing, but being a part of this natural process."

When designing a contemplative outdoor space, Trutza recommends considering the design parameters of intimacy and scale to create a space that has the essence of a refuge. "It should draw us into the space and beckon us to stay," he says.

Trutza says the elements that are most often used in meditation spaces are the sounds of a gentle fountain to mask unwanted sounds, some sort of shade either natural or man-made, and comfortable outdoor furniture. "However, a mistake that can be made is to incorporate too many disparate design elements that can create confusion visually," he says. "The whole point is to center the mind and nourish a sense of well-being. Avoid clutter and trying to be an overachiever by combining too many elements."

For those who want to focus on a Zen meditation space, which is often more efficient in terms of simplicity, Trutza offers these tips: 1) restraint is the key when it comes to the number and type of elements included in a Zen space—follow the "less is more" principal, 2) create order and thoughtful, controlled placement of objects within the space,

and 3) use texture and contrasting plant forms that allow appreciation of nature's inherent beauty.

"Moreover," concludes Trutza, "a spiritual calm and reverence should define any contemplative space by incorporating the same principles— soothing, peaceful, and introspective."

ABOVE: *Elements such as water, plants, shade, and sky work together to create a tranquil, thought-provoking atmosphere.*
OPPOSITE: *Some people believe that walking a labyrinth, like this one outlined by rocks, will bring quietude and stillness of mind by the time you reach the middle of the circular path.*

The act of putting into your mouth what the earth has grown is perhaps your most direct interaction with the earth.

FRANCES MOORE LAPPÉ

ENTERTAINING ALFRESCO

Celebrating Your Garden and Its Harvest

~

There is little more satisfying than enjoying a meal out-of-doors. The fresh air and the sounds of nature conspire naturally to relax the body and mind. Whether it is a sunrise breakfast alone on your terrace or a feast for fifty on your wrap-around porch, the effect is the same. When spending time outside, the act of eating becomes a joy to be appreciated, savored, and shared.

Many people long to dine outside or throw a party that utilizes their outdoor space. But oftentimes it is thought to be too difficult or time consuming, and therefore, the tendency is to rely on the home's interior spaces. The reality is that although there is some additional planning involved, it is no more difficult to prepare a meal or host a party outside than in. By taking advantage of your outdoor space, dining alfresco may become your preferred way of living.

If your outdoor living space includes a fully stocked exterior kitchen, a wood-burning pizza oven, or a free-standing barbeque grill, you have the tools necessary to cook your meals outside. A table or sideboard placed on your porch or an antique wooden farm table in the middle of your courtyard can serve as a buffet, dessert table, or bar. A brightly colored tablecloth, some flickering candlelight, and an arrangement of flowers from your garden are all that is needed to set the scene for dining open air.

Outdoor dining is enhanced when sharing the stage with a crackling fire, a flowing fountain, lush vegetation, and a cool night breeze.

Even more rewarding is that the essential ingredients for many recipes can be grown in your own yard. Gardens can host a vast array of herbs, vegetables, fruits, and even edible flowers that greatly enhance your gastronomic experience. Many of us pay extra for those grocery items designated as homegrown or organic, so planting the produce we use most in a small plot next to our outdoor kitchen can benefit the senses as well as please the palate.

Whether or not you are able to create your own cooking garden, just taking the opportunity to experience your meals outside will add a new dimension to your everyday life. Putting it all together and entertaining outdoors can become a gift of the heart and home.

Entertaining in the Southwest

~

Some of the most memorable parties take place outdoors. Majestic mountains, cool pines, or the serene desert—the Southwest offers an unforgettable backdrop for entertaining in the open air. "Planning your event with the outdoors in mind can inspire your creativity and can greatly enhance the experience," believes David Bauer, owner of the Phoenix, Arizona-based event planning company, The Director. Bauer offers the following advice for successful outdoor entertaining.

If your dining area is far away from the kitchen, and especially if dining on roof decks, plan to have all your items and menu there at one time so you aren't continually leaving the party to fetch food and drink. Also, you should know that entertaining outdoors takes a little more time for preparation, because you are most likely moving a lot of things from inside your home to the outdoors. Give yourself an extra half hour of time to set up.

ABOVE: *Dining on a high-rise balcony offers exhilarating views of the cityscape at sunset.*
RIGHT: *For easy and enjoyable entertaining, a serving bar sits poolside enveloped by the sounds of the waterfall and the cooling effects of mist.*

Plan for the party to have a flow rather than be focused in one spot. Place food or drink stations in the front courtyard, side yard, and back patio so people will move about, giving them a reason to mingle and meet others.

To provide additional lighting, use votive candleholders on stakes to illuminate the area. Placing them right next to sprinklers can serve as an effective safeguard against guests tripping.

Don't be afraid to use your nice china, silver, and linen napkins outside—it makes a dramatic statement in the garden setting. Also, try using natural and casual décor like wicker baskets, potted plants as centerpieces, or a variety of mixed glasses and plates. The outdoor setting is the perfect place to be creative and do the unexpected.

A cool evening breeze and the subtle shimmer of the pool create the perfect ambiance for an outdoor wine and cheese party.

If you plan to use an outdoor fire feature, make sure it is lit at least thirty minutes before guests arrive so it welcomes the early arrivals in full, crackling swing.

Music, music, music! Music is the key to entertaining. Whether it's Mozart or rock n' roll, whatever you choose, be sure to turn on the music before guests arrive to help set the tone for the party. If you have the gentle sounds of nature as your music, set the volume low.

If you are hosting more than ten guests, spend a few extra dollars and hire help. Have them come one hour before the party and stay one hour after. Not only will you be able to enjoy your guests, but also when you wake up in the morning, you'll realize how wonderful it is to have a clean kitchen—inside and out.

Above all, be flexible and don't panic! If the weather doesn't cooperate, stop a moment and realize that there is a way to handle it without all your plans being drenched. Remember, almost anything you can do outside, you can do inside—and vice versa.

ABOVE: *There is something enchanting about dining outdoors under the moon and the stars.* RIGHT: *When dining poolside, use plastic glasses and plates to minimize possible accidents with broken glass.*

LEFT: *Confetti salad is beautiful and delicious when made with your own garden bounty.* ABOVE: *There is nothing more impressive than creating a meal with your own produce. Using Linda's recipes, make this herbed oil goat cheese appetizer with fresh roasted potatoes.*

Quick Garden Goodies from the Kitchen Herbalist

~

Try these simple and easy recipes using items from your own garden. It is so much fun to walk outside, select your ingredients, and then create your meal without ever leaving home!

HERBED OLIVE OIL APPETIZERS: Take a good quality olive oil and add chopped fresh herbs and flowers from your garden such as garlic chives, chive flowers, lemon balm, thyme, nasturtiums, calendula petals, rosemary, or dianthus flower petals. Sprinkle with sea salt and fresh ground pepper. Drizzle on your favorite goat cheese and/or serve with slices of crusty French bread.

ROASTED HERBED POTATOES: Slice red or Yukon Gold potatoes into wedges and put in a large bowl. Add chopped fresh rosemary or dill, minced fresh garlic, salt, and pepper, and then drizzle a little olive oil over them. Toss to evenly coat all wedges and spread them out on a cookie sheet in a single layer. Cook in a 375° oven until browned, about one hour. Try serving the potatoes with sour cream that has a little fresh garlic, lemon juice, fresh dill, salt, and pepper.

CONFETTI SALAD: Start with a nice green salad mix. Add a variety of fresh herbs such as basil, dill, Italian parsley, spearmint, chervil, tarragon, and garlic chives. To bring beautiful color into your salad, add petals of calendula, petals of blue bachelor buttons, nasturtium flowers, or violas. Top with your favorite vinaigrette.

Beautiful Beverages
~

When you are adding fresh herbs and flowers to your dinner entrées, don't forget the beverages! There are just as many wonderful ways to enhance your libations as your dining delights.

WONDERFUL WATER: To a pitcher of water, add five or six sprigs of fresh mint (try spearmint, orange mint, or pineapple mint) and a few edible flowers such as dianthus, pink clove (carnation), or violas. Or, try adding fresh rose petals for a really romantic appeal.

UNFORGETTABLE ICE: Fill ice cube trays with filtered water and add to each spot a little viola or baby sprig of mint. Freeze and use in cold beverages as usual. Or, to create an unforgettable ice ring for your next party, add fresh flowers and herbs along with fresh fruit slices to the water. Freeze and then add to the punch.

FRESH HERB TEA: There are an infinite number of herbal tea combinations you can make. As a rule of thumb, steep your teas, covered, for about fifteen to twenty-five minutes. Strain and add additional water until you reach your desired strength. A flavorful tea can be made by blending fresh spearmint, cinnamon sticks, black tea (or herbal "black tea"), and honey to taste. Or, try combining fresh lemon balm, lemon verbena, alfalfa, and either licorice mint or orange mint. Your guests will never believe that many of the ingredients came from your own garden!

ABOVE: *Add color and interest to your beverages by using fresh herbs or veggies from your own garden.*
OPPOSITE: *When the weather cooperates, move your meal out into your garden and experience the feeling of freedom it provides.*

AROMATIC PLANTS

~

The Southwest climate can host a tremendous number of plants that produce pleasing,
sometimes intoxicating, aromas. The following list is just a sampling.

AROMATIC FOLIAGE

TREES/SHRUBS

Arizona cypress tree *(Cupressus arizonica)*

Artemesia, varieties *(Artemeia spp.)*

Basil, varieties *(Ocimum spp.)*

Bay laurel/sweet bay *(Laurus nobilis)*

Creosote *(Larrea tridentate)*

Desert lavender *(Hyptis emoryi)*

Eucalyptus trees, varieties *(Eucalyptus spp.)*

Germander *(Teucrium chamaedrys)*

Lemon verbena *(Aloysia triphylla)*

Mexican tarragon *(Tagetes lucida)*

Mountain marigold *(Tagetes palmeri)*

Oregano: Mexican *(Lippia graveolens)* & Sonoran
   (Lippia palmeri)

Pine trees: Afghan *(Pinus eldarica)* & Aleppo
   (Pinus halepensis)

Popcorn cassia *(cassia didymobotrya)*

Rosemary, varieties *(Rosemarinus spp.)*

Sage/Salvia, varieties *(Salvia spp.)*

Santolina/Lavender cotton: gray-leaved
   (Santolina chamaecyparissus) & green-leaved
   (Santolina virens)

Scented geranium, many varieties
   (Pelargonium spp.)

Whitebrush/Bee brush *(Aloysia gratissima)*

SMALL SHRUBS/CONTAINER PLANTS/GROUNDCOVERS/ANNUALS

Curry plant *(Helichrysum italicum)*

Devil's claw *(Proboscidea parviflora var. hohokamiana)*

Fennel *(Foeniculum vulgare)*

Mint, varieties *(Mentha spp.)*

Oregano/marjoram, many varieties
   (Origanum spp.)

Sage/Salvia: Pineapple sage *(Salvia elegans)* &
   Garden sage *(Salvia officinalis)*

Savory: Winter *(Satureja montana)* & Summer
   (Satureja hortensis)

Sweet Annie *(Artemesia annua)*

Thyme, varieties *(Thymus spp)*

AROMATIC FLOWERS

TREES/SHRUBS

Acacia, many varieties *(Acacia spp.)*

African sumac *(Rhus lancea)*

Anacacho orchid tree *(Bauhinia lunaroides)*

Cassia/Senna *(Cassia spp.)*

Citrus, any variety *(Citrus spp.)*

Desert willow *(Chilopsis linearis)*

Ebony: Texas *(Pithecelobium flexicaule)* & Mexican
   (Pithecelobium mexicanum)

Flowering plums, varieties *(Prunus spp.)*

Gardenia *(Gardenia jasminoides)*

Mexican Jumping-Bean *(Sapium biloculare)*

Natal plum *(Carissa grandiflora)*

Roses, most varieties *(Rosa spp.)*

Smoke Tree *(Psorothamnus spinosus)*

Southern magnolia *(Magnolia grandiflora)*

Texas Mountain Laurel *(Sophora secundiflora)*

SCENTED GRASSES

Lemongrass, varieties *(Cymbopogon spp.)*

Vanilla grass *(Hierochloe odorata)*

ANNUAL FLOWERS

Balm/mint/bergamot *(Monarda spp.)*

Candytuft *(Iberis amara)*

Four o'clocks *(Mirabilis jalapa)*

Stock, varieties *(Matthiola spp.)*

Sweet pea (vine) *(Lathyrus odoratus)*

Sweety alyssum *(Lobularia maritime)*

PERENNIAL FLOWERS

Ajo lily *(Hesperocallis undulata)*

Blackfood daisy *(Melampodium leucanthum)*

Chocolate flower *(Berlandieri lyrata)*

Desert phlox *(Phlox tennuifolia)*

Dianthus, pink *(Dianthus plumarius)*

Evening primrose *(Oenothera caespitosa)*

Goodding verbena *(Verbena gooddingi)*

Palmer's penstemon *(Penstemon palmeri)*

WATER GARDEN/POND PLANTS

Fragrant white flowers *(Yerba mansa)*

Mint, varieties *(Mentha spp.)*

VINES

Hyacinth bean/Lab-lab vine *(Dolichos lablab)*

Lady Banks' Rose, white-flowering only *(Rosa
   banksiae 'Alba Plena')*

Star Jasmine *(Trachelospermum jasminoides)*

CACTI

Easter lily cactus *(Echinopsis multiplex)*

Night-blooming cereus/Arizona queen-of-
   the-night *(Peniocereus greggii)*

BIBLIOGRAPHY
~

Arizona Master Gardeners. *Desert Landscaping for Beginners.* Ed. Cathy Cromell. Phoenix, AZ: Arizona Master Gardener Press in cooperation with The University of Arizona Maricopa County Cooperative Extension. 2001.

Arizona Native Plant Society, Urban Landscape Committee. *Desert Accent Plants.* Tucson, AZ: Arizona Native Plant Society. 1992.

Arizona Native Plant Society, Urban Landscape Committee. *Desert Bird Gardening.* Tucson, AZ: Arizona Native Plant Society. 1997.

Arizona Native Plant Society, Urban Landscape Committee. *Desert Butterfly Gardening.* Tucson, AZ: Arizona Native Plant Society. 1996.

Arizona Native Plant Society, Urban Landscape Committee. *Desert Ground Covers and Vines.* Tucson, AZ: Arizona Native Plant Society. 1991.

Arizona Native Plant Society, Urban Landscape Committee. *Desert Shrubs.* Tucson, AZ: Arizona Native Plant Society. 1990.

Arizona Native Plant Society, Urban Landscape Committee. *Desert Wildflowers.* Tucson, AZ: Arizona Native Plant Society. 1991.

Cromell, Cathy; Guy, Linda A.; and Bradley, Lucy K. *Desert Gardening for Beginners.* Phoenix, AZ: Arizona Master Gardener Press in cooperation with The University of Arizona Maricopa County Cooperative Extension. 1999.

Epple, Ann Orth. *A Field Guide to the Plants of Arizona.* Helena, MT: Falcon Publishing, Inc. 1995.

Fenzl, Barbara Pool. *Savor the Southwest.* San Francisco, CA: Bay Books. 1999.

Fenzl, Barbara Pool. *Southwest the Beautiful Cookbook.* San Francisco, CA: Harper Collins Publishers. 1994.

Gardening in the Desert. Tucson, AZ: The University of Arizona Press. 2000.

Irish, Mary. *Arizona Gardener's Guide.* Nashville, TN: Cool Springs Press. 2002.

Mielke, Judy. *Native Plants for Southwestern Landscapes.* Austin, Texas: University of Texas Press. 1993.

Sunset Editorial Staff. *Sunset Western Garden Annual, 2002 Edition.* Menlo Park, CA: Sunset Publishing Corporation. 2002.

Sunset Editorial Staff. *Sunset Western Landscaping.* Ed. Kathleen Norris Brenzel. Menlo Park, CA: Sunset Publishing Corporation. 1997.

Sunset Editorial Staff. *Western Garden Book.* Ed. Kathleen Norris Brenzel. Menlo Park, CA: Sunset Publishing Corporation. 2001.

Yoder, Sylvia. *Desert Hummingbird Gardens.* Paradise Valley, AZ: Real Estate Consulting and Education, Inc. 1999.

RESOURCES

~

SHANNON BREHMER ALLSWORTH
Phoenix, AZ
602/426-9350
shannonallsworth@yahoo.com

TROY BANKORD
Environmental Design, Landscape Construction
Consultation & Maintenance
T.M. Bankord, Inc.
Phoenix, AZ
602/482-6852

DAVID BAUER
Owner & Event Planner
The Director, LLC.
Phoenix, AZ
602/840-9011

JULIA BERMAN
Owner & Landscape Designer
Julia Berman Design
Santa Fe, NM
505/820-3314

LUCY K. BRADLEY
Extension Agent, Urban Horticulture
The University of Arizona
Cooperative Extension
Phoenix, AZ
602/470-8086
BradleyL@ag.arizona.edu
http://cals.arizona.edu/maricopa/garden/

BEVERLY BURCH
Owner
The Willows at Hilton Village
Scottsdale, AZ
480/348-9599

AMY CARLILE
Partner
Southwest Gardener
Phoenix, AZ
602/279-9510
info@southwestgardener.com
www.southwestgardener.com

NANCY CHRISTENSEN
Managing Editor & Garden Editor
Phoenix Home & Garden
Scottsdale, AZ
480/664-3960
800/228-6540
phg@citieswestpub.com
www.phgmag.com

CORNELL LAB OF ORNITHOLOGY
Ithaca, NY
607/254-2473
www.birds.cornell.edu

JOE COTITTA
Photographer
Epic Multimedia
Scottsdale, AZ
480/607-1862
joe@epicplaces.com
www.epicplaces.com

JENNIE CURÉ
Landscape Architect
Eden West Studio & Garden
Cave Creek, AZ
480/595-8616
jennie@jenniecure.com
www.jenniecure.com

LISA DELL'OSSO
Partner & Designer
Cathedral Interiors
San Francisco, CA
415/665-8895
Paradise Valley, AZ
480/367-0956

LINDA ENGER
Photographer
Linda Enger Photography
Phoenix, AZ
602/271-9503
linda@lindaengerphoto.com
http://www.lindaengerphoto.com

BARBARA POOL FENZL
Owner, Teacher, & Author
Les Gourmettes Cooking School
Phoenix, AZ
602/240-6767

JOE FOSTER
Spa Consultant
Durango Stoves, Spas & More
Durango, CO
970/247-8716

JEFFREY GREEN
Photographer
Jeffrey Green Photography
Las Vegas, NV & Phoenix, AZ
800/257-4347
702/257-1655
jgreenphoto@cox.net
www.jgreenphoto.com

ACKNOWLEDGEMENTS

~

I have been privileged to work with some extraordinary people on the creation of this book. The experience deepened my respect for those who take to heart the concept of outdoor living space.

Many, many thanks to Tammy Gales, my editor at Northland Publishing, who has been a valued partner on this journey. Her advice and direction is so very appreciated. And to David Jenney and Katie Jennings, I give thanks for their creativity and ingenuity in designing this exceptional book.

To Nancy Christensen, garden editor at *Phoenix Home and Garden*, and to the magazine's staff, I give my utmost thanks for the unwavering support, and for the discovery of many of these unique outdoor spaces.

Deep gratitude goes to Catherine Ross, a friend and coach, who helped guide me on this path when life's inevitable obstacles would arise.

To Eileen Bailey, friend and mentor, I give my love and continued thanks for her insight, wisdom, and guidance. Her confidence in my abilities has taken me from my first writing assignment more than ten years ago to the completion of this project.

Thank you to the professionals who have offered their suggestions on how we can all live better lives when we embrace our outdoor living space. The world is a better place because of your hard work.

I am amazed by the art of the contributing photographers. With their skill and attention to detail, we can all enjoy the spectacular images of design and nature.

Thanks, too, to friend and colleague Mary La Russo, whose sense of style has benefited not only some of the exquisite photographs contained in this book, but also the countless features she managed while at *The Arizona Republic*.

Dense foliage provides shade and privacy for reading or daydreaming.

To the late Ann Wright-Edwards, a dear friend and counselor, I send my love and thoughts daily. Together with Ginger Hutton and the Storytellers, Ann inspired in me a new and deeper passion for writing.

My family and friends have been exemplary in their heartfelt support and encouragement. Thanks go to all of you who have helped in countless ways—Martie, Paulina, Shelly, Lisa, Pamela, Stacey, Sara, Pam, Julia, Gloria, Monica, Marcia, Meridith, Shannon, Sharisse, Paul, Range, Aimee, Julie, Danielle, Daphne, Suzanne, Alex, and Jaime.

To my husband, John, who continues to go above and beyond what is expected in his love, support, and encouragement, I give my everlasting love and deep admiration. And to our son Neo, and daughter Eco, I offer you both the joy that a cherished outdoor space can bring to the soul and the love of a lifetime.